D1598916

RICHMINDED

THE KEYS TO SUCCESS
THE KEYS TO BUILDING WEALTH
THE KEYS TO BUILDING AN EMPIRE

RASHAN LAWHORNE

Richminded Academy

5 Concourse Pkwy

Atlanta GA 30328

http://richminded.net

Ordering Information:

Quantity sales. Special discounts are available on quantity purchases by corporations, associations, and others. For details, contact the publisher at the address above.

Printed in the United States of America

First Printing, 2017

ISBN 978-0-692-89987-8

Richminded Academy

5 Concourse Pkwy

Atlanta GA 30328

http://richminded.net

Dedication

This book is dedicated to my foundation—my family, who is responsible for my growth and for whom I strive to be successful for everyday.

My uncle & aunts, who showed me the keys to entrepreneurship.

My sister and brother, who believed in my dreams, my parents who showed me the real meaning of love, and all my Hustlers and Hustlettes out there working on their dreams daily to succeed and build wealth for their families.

I especially dedicate this book to my wife, who keeps pushing me higher to success daily.

Contents

Introduction

Everybody Is Not Ballin'
Most is Fallin'
Even More Is Crawlin'
When They Look Up,
All They See Is The Position Y'all In
So Don't Be So Up
That It'll Blind You
And So Far Ahead That You
Don't See The People Behind You
Help People Succeed And You
Will Definitely See Success

The reason I wrote this book, Richminded, is because not enough of us are saving money, investing our earnings, putting our money away to work for us, starting businesses, teaching our kids how to create wealth, supporting each other, or coming together to start empires.

We have to get our mind right, own something, build generational wealth, build a circle of friends that will uplift us, support us, help us, and hold us accountable. We have to produce wealth, plan for the future, travel, build families, and do whatever it takes to Hustle hard for success.

We are grown now. We have to start doing grown-up things.

We can get so much accomplished if we stop spending so much time turning up, hating on each other, glorifying negativity, following everything the media says, trying to impress people who do not care, not supporting each other, blaming others, worrying, listening to dream killers and brainwashing ourselves that success can't happen. We have to do what it takes to succeed to build an empire.

I wanted to write a book that would uplift you, help your spirit grow, motivate you to fulfill your purpose, help you build a business, and help you on your life journey. We complain daily but do we support each other? Do we try to build with each other? Do we try and come together and purchase property? Do we have faith in each other? Do we trust each other to do business? Do we pay attention when other people present us opportunities? Do we put our funds together to invest or build?

Do we invest in ourselves? Do we mentor the youth and tell them what is wrong? Do we mentor them for entrepreneurship? Are we trying to build families together? Are we teaching our young ladies that being half-naked on social media is wrong? Are we actually trying to open businesses and clean up our communities? Are we holding each other accountable for the nonsense that goes on, including negative rappers and sites on the internet that show us in a bad light. Are we trying to become law enforcement so we can put more of us in our communities to help balance it out? Do we even know what entrepreneurship is? Are we protesting to change the high single mother rate in our communities.

Why do we glorify gangsters, gangs, drugs, crime, and negativity? Are we boycotting the radio and media who share negative images of us daily? Are we on social media acting a fool instead of using this technology to build wealth? Do we protest when our people are killing each other over dumb stuff? Do you even shop with your own people? Are you really ready for an economic shutdown?

Facts: In 2011 when I lost my last Job, I was paid 30k a year plus commission. That was the 3rd job I lost due to corporate downsizing in the last 6 years.

There were no jobs out there. Unemployment was only $330 a week. It wouldn't even cover my mortgage, let alone anything else. I was desperate not to lose my house and cars, to keep the lights and the day-care bills paid, so I turned to the streets. After getting caught up in a case and not wanting to rely on the streets or a job again, I started teaching myself the hidden gems of becoming an entrepreneur.

In 2012, I tripled my income and made over $100,000 when I became an entrepreneur. I've never looked back to the streets or a job again. This is why I go so hard on entrepreneurship.

All I want is financial independence for people.

I want us to open more businesses so that we can create more jobs for ourselves. I want us to stop supporting people that run over us, disrespect us, and prey on us. I want us to stop being brokeminded and start thinking bigger.

I want us to stop making other people rich, stop building other people's dreams, and get more worth for our precious little time. I want us to start creating wealth for our families. I want us to recognize that these entrepreneurship opportunities that are presented to change lives are not a scam, a hustle, or a con like the slave masters taught your whole family to believe. I want us to recognize that slow broke thinking has been passed down to us.

I want us to save, invest, go all out for success, travel, do better, and live a great life. I also want us to open up healthy businesses so that they can stop killing us slowly with all this fast food, soda, junk food, dirty fried chicken places, and very unhealthy establishments in our neighborhoods. I also want us to open more hair and beauty product stores.

Last, I just want us to support each other and stop focusing on celebs and everybody else that don't give a damn about us. That's all I'm trying to make your feel in this book. I am just tired of people being financially in last place!

Believe

ALWAYS BELIEVE IN YOURSELF AND SUCCESS WILL ALWAYS FOLLOW YOU.

IF YOU DO NOT BELIEVE IN YOURSELF TO BE GREATER, OR DO NOT BELIEVE IN YOUR DREAMS, THEN WHO WILL?

Voice to Tom Brady: you need a field goal, two touchdowns and two 2 point conversions in ONE QUARTER to take this to overtime. That's IMPOSSIBLE!!!

Tom Brady: Let's get to work then! We got this!

If you believe in yourself to win NOTHING IS IMPOSSIBLE!

If you do not believe in yourself to be greater, or do not believe in your dreams, then who will?

Believe Even When They Don't

When I was 10 years old, my teacher went around my entire classroom, asking each kid to write down and to share what they wanted to be when they grew up.

Most of the kids said things like.....Police Officers....Firemen....School Teachers, Doctors, Movie Stars, Musicians etc. I wrote down that I wanted to be a BOSS.

My teacher called me up to the front of the class. When I arrived at the front of the class, she said, "Rashan, now why would you write that you wanted to be a BOSS? Has anyone from your neighborhood EVER been a BOSS? Has anyone from your FAMILY ever been a Boss? Do you know ANYone who has ever been a Boss? Yes? No?

I think the answer is no, so WHY would you write that down if you know absolutely nothing about being a Boss?!"

So I said, "Ms. Dreamkiller, in the future they will be inventing something called the internet. We will have access to millions of people via something called social media. We will have handheld smartphones which will be miniature handheld computers. I will have the capability to not only become my own boss, but be able to make an infinite amount of money that you can only dream of from any location of my choosing."

She told me I was a smartass with a crazy imagination and then called my mother on me.

Business

I HEAR PEOPLE ALL THE TIME SAY TO ME, "I DON'T HAVE THE MONEY TO START A BUSINESS." THEY ARE NOT INFORMED THAT, WITH ALL THIS TECHNOLOGY, YOU DON'T NEED ANYTHING BUT A WILL TO WIN.

How to open a business for under $1

Sit down and really think about what your gift is and what your passion in life is. It could be training or coaching others, selling apparel, selling services, being an author, selling goods, doing offiine services etc. Whatever you have a talent for

1. You will need a domain name. Google a 99 cent domain name from godaddy for whatever you like to do or have a gift for.

2. Open social media accounts for that brand FREE

Example: YouTube, Twitter, FB, Instagram, Snapchat, LinkedIn etc. Open a YouTube channel for your brand, Twitter account, Facebook page, free blogging page and IG page for whatever your business will be and start marketing your business and building your online following. All of this super technology is free, free, free. There are 7 billion consumers (and counting) out there.

3. Use Wix for a FREE website

4. Open a account with paypal or stripe for a FREE merchant account

5. Use the 3 billion consumers online to push your passion for FREE

6. Pray. God doesn't charge. His time is FREE!

Bonus* Go get a FREE EIN number for your new business Go to irs.gov and get a free EIN # to solidly your business and visualize it. You can Inc it later when you start making money.

Simple as that. You are holding your own self from greatness. I hear people all the time say to me, "I don't have the money to start a business." They are not informed that with all this technology, you don't need anything but a will to win.

You are going to struggle at first. You are going to see people that were down with you for years not support you. You are going to question your decision to go after your dream.

There are going to be a few sleepless nights because you are worrying about producing income. People will make snide remarks and hate on you because you are trying to do big things. At some point, you are going to want to give up, but I PROMISE in the end you will feel better about yourself.

You will make tons more $$$, have more time for family, and you will have the last laugh on anyone who ever doubted you.

Here is a list of businesses that you can start RIGHT NOW!

Business Consultant, Event Planner, Become an Author, Open a Clothing Line, Food Delivery Service, Event DJ, Personal Trainer, Tax Preparer, Home Improvement, Auto Broker, Graphic Design, Computer Repair, Household Services (lawn, carpet cleaning, maid etc), Hairstylist, Open a Barber Shop, Restaurant or Food Truck, Juice Bar, Music or Dance Lessons, Small Biz Marketing, Photography, Real Estate & Flipping Houses, Buying and reselling on eBay, Day Care, Pet sitting, travel agency, auto detailing, baking and decorating, Cleaning services for businesses, Handyman services, Hiring agency, Catering, Senior citizen assistance, tutoring, become a business or life coach, Website Design, Uber, whatever your passion is, or the same thing you do at your job for 8 hours daily to make other people rich.

Stop with all the excuses. Excuses will always keep you broke & struggling.

Make 6 Figures On The Internet

Get 500 people to buy a $200 product.

Get 1,000 people to buy a $100 product.

Get 2,000 people to buy a $50 product.

Can't sell a product? Then sell a service!

Get 500 people to pay $17 a month, for 1 yr

Get 200 people to pay $42 a month, for 1 yr

Get 100 people to pay $83 a month, for 1 yr

There are a billion consumers online. Go get it!

Start a Mobile Business

Here are some Mobile Business ideas to generate income:

- Mobile Hair Dresser/Barber/Cosmetologist

- Mobile Mechanic or Detail Service

- Mobile Personal Training

- Mobile Food Delivery or Mobile Restaurant

- Mobile Personal Supermarket shopping

- Mobile Pharmacy pickup/dropoff for elderly

- Mobile Pet grooming/pet sitting/walking or pet salon

- Mobile Home Cleaning Services - Maid, Landscape, Carpet cleaning, power washing etc

- Mobile Tutor

- Mobile CPU services

- Mobile Repair

- Mobile Photography

I can go on and on. There are plenty of things that you can do to make money. You just have to put trust in yourself to make it work.

Don't Start a Business To Make Money

Never join or start a business just to "make money." Start a business to make a difference! The money will follow.

Most of Us Are Starting Behind

Most of us are 10+ years behind in this business world. We are in last place when it comes to finances. If business ethics, entrepreneurship , and business models would have been instilled in us at an earlier age like 16,17, or 18, it would have sparked ideas to paths that could have been executed by age 21 and beyond.

On the contrary, most of us did not become business inclined, for whatever reason, on a decent foundation until our early-mid 20s and many in their 30s and 40s.

I am saying this because there is NO time for play. Time's up. NO room for error. Be decisive with all things. NO ideas to be held upon out of fear. Stop doubting yourself.

There's no time to be wasted focusing on the next man or woman's journey and no time for playing and hating. It's time to execute, timely, precisely, with hard work, and go all out for success. There is no time for a pity party. You don't have time for would have, could have, or should have.

It's time to live with your eyes wide open, focused in on the goals, with less talking and more working, less stunting and more growing, less hate of yourself and other people, and more repairing from within and supporting each other.

Determination

I GUARANTEE IF YOU KEEP PUSHING FORWARD, BELIEVE IN YOURSELF, AND GO ALL OUT FOR YOUR DREAMS DESPITE YOUR HARDSHIPS, YOU CAN OWN YOUR OWN EMPIRE AND FIX YOUR LIFE!

Oprah Winfrey wore potato sacks because clothing did not always fit into the budget of her poverty-stricken family. She grew up around extreme poverty and endured years of sexual and physical abuse.

Iyanla Vanzant lost her daughter to cancer, was raped as a child, was on welfare, was a single teen mom struggling to survive, had her marriage end in divorce, and also lost her home to foreclosure. Any other person in her shoes would have given up hope.

Oprah Winfrey became the first black female news anchor before the age of 20 in Nashville, but she wanted to give up because she was sexually harassed, humiliated, and ultimately FIRED!!

Iyanla Vanzant contemplated suicide, but prayed on it and realized she had a purpose in this world to turn pain into progress.

Now Oprah Winfrey is called the Queen of All Media, has been ranked the richest African-American and the greatest black philanthropist in American history. She is currently North America's first and only multi-billionaire black person worth 3 BILLION dollars.

Iyanla Vanzant has turned her pain into helping others. She is an inspirational speaker, lawyer, spiritual minister, author, life coach and television personality. She is known primarily for her books, of which she has sold over a million, and has her own show which helps fixes broken relationships and mental instability. She is frequently featured as a guest teacher of Oprah's Lifeclass on the Oprah Winfrey Network and has millions of followers.

I guarantee if you keep pushing forward, believe in yourself and go all out for your dreams despite your hardships you can OWN your own empire and FIX YOUR LIFE!

Stick With Your Dream

Taraji P. Henson became pregnant with her son during her junior year of college. Her no-getter family and friends advised her to drop-out. They figured that it would be impossible for her to finish school as a single mother.

She carried her son to every class with her. When she graduated from Howard University, she carried her son across the stage to pick up her degree.

Following college, she moved from D.C. to L.A. with a 2-year old baby, and $700.00 to her name.

She struggled for YEARS through bit parts, low pay, side jobs, welfare assistance, etc. Her father told her that she was crazy, and pushed her to come home, but she STUCK WITH HER DREAM!!

Today she is the star of one of the highest-rated shows on television. She is landing leading roles in Oscar nominated movies. She owns six properties, and she is a multi-millionaire.

Have a vision for your life? GO for it. Don't listen to these DREAM-KILLERS. NEVER give up!!!

The Difference Between Winners and Losers

A winner is just a loser who tried one more time! Never give up! Turn your negatives into a positive.

Keep Pushing

If you start your own business do not quit after NOT seeing results because you posted it on your social media pages a few times. Your friends & family will not support that aspect of your life no matter how hard you try. They are not built for that.

But if you keep pushing, pray on it, and hustle your ass off with the 3 billion consumers online, I promise you will make more money and have more financial freedom than you have ever had in your life. Please also stop worrying about what other people will think because you have yet to see them deliver a check to your mailbox.

Never stop grinding! Your breakthrough is coming. Some will. Some won't. So what? By any means do not quit or give up. There are too many haters hoping you will FAIL.

Get Rich or Die Crying

You should NOT quit on your VISION based off these no-gettas inability to see it. Don't let a 30k a year mentality keep you from making 30k a month.

You Are 3 Feet from Gold

I know it seems like it's not going to work out or your success is not moving quick enough but the truth is your delay is not a denial. You just have to keep digging. It's coming. You are 3 feet from gold.

Don't give up and, most importantly, don't let unsupportive people stop your shine.

Dreams

IF YOU HAVEN'T FELT LIKE QUITTING, YOUR DREAMS AREN'T BIG ENOUGH. **S**URROUND YOURSELF WITH PEOPLE WHO DREAM BIGGER THAN YOU!

If you haven't felt like quitting, your dreams aren't big enough. Surround yourself with people who dream bigger than you!

Don't Procrastinate

Every day you procrastinate on your million-dollar-a-year dream, you lose $2,739.72. As long as you are ALIVE, it is NEVER too late to follow your DREAMS, and there is no time like the PRESENT to get STARTED.

Dreams Don't Come Easily

Listen.... don't think for a moment putting yourself out there and going after your dreams is going to be easy. You will lose friends, family will give you the side eye, people you think have your back will turn away from you. You will have to listen to people tell you to get a job or keep your job. You will barely get support.

You will get dream killers in your ear telling you to quit and telling you it won't work. HATERS will come at you with their negative, condescending, smartass comments. You will also learn that strangers will support you more than family and friends ever will.

But if you keep pushing and go all out to make your dreams come true, I promise your life will change for the better. You will feel better about life. You will have a renewed faith in yourself. You will get paid exactly what you are worth.

Don't let these people stop you. They wish they had the courage and heart you have to go after success.

When you first share your dream with people, they'll tell you that you can never achieve it. When you start working towards your dream, they'll ask why are wasting your time doing that. When you finally achieve your dream, they'll ask you how you did it.

Never let anyone's negativity and small vision keep you from your goals and dreams!

Don't Sleep On Your Dreams

Ladies....you could be making a lot of money by utilizing YouTube. I know many people who are making a life-changing income from making videos. You can do makeup tutorials, cooking shows, fitness, fashion tips, life and relationship coaching, hair and beauty, financial training, music, your own reality shows, or just use your talents to think outside the box.

The best part about YouTube is its free. You can make 100 videos a day and get charged $0.00.

Don't sleep on YouTube.

Don't sleep on your dreams, either.

Your Job Is No Excuse

I don't care how special you think your JOB is or how much you make there. I don't care how long you've been there or that you are a manager, supervisor, in a union, best friends with the boss, hang out with the Human Resources lady, on the verge of a promotion, or just comfortable because you are paid for your time every other Friday.

That gives you no excuse not to want to build your own dream, no excuse not to look into something that will make you extra income, and no excuse not to support your friends or family that think differently from you and run their own time. Let's be better than that!

Don't Be a Waiter or Waitress

There are a lot of Waiters and Waitresses in the world. They wait and wait and wait and wait for something to come their way, for a job to fall in their laps, a raise, money to fall from the sky, a loan to go through, a credit card to come in the mail, tax return season, or an opportunity to knock on their door. These things will never come because they don't realize that they have to go out and make opportunities happen.

A real go-getter waits for nothing. We take action, go after success, make plans, and follow through. I cannot stress this enough.

Every day work on your vision, your masterplan, your goals and all your dreams, or you will be hired at a very low wage to execute someone else's.

Don't Give People the Power to Starve You

I'm going to break it down the very best I can for you as far as building your own dreams. It's very simple. If you give people the power to feed you, then you also give the same people the power to starve you.

Doubts Kill Dreams

Fact: Doubts kill more dreams than failure ever will. Never let someone who gave up on their dreams talk you out of yours.

Make Your Goals and Dreams BIGGER!

Remember how you used to feel back in grade school or middle school when you received some fresh new gear? You struggled to sleep, and you couldn't WAIT to get up BRIGHT and EARLY, because you were ANXIOUS to ROCK that new gear.

Sleep almost felt like......a DISTRACTION!

That is how you feel EVERY MORNING when your GOALS and your AMBITIONS are in order!!! The problem is NOT that you are not a morning person.

The PROBLEM is that your GOALS and your DREAMS are not BIG enough, so you have nothing to look FORWARD to!!!! You betta GET UP, GET OUT, and GET something!

Don't let the days of your life pass you by! You betta GET UP, GET OUT, and GET something, cause you and I gotta do for you and I!!!

Entrepreneurship

ENTREPRENEURSHIP DOES NOT BEGIN MERELY WHEN YOUR BUSINESS IS OFFICIALLY ESTABLISHED & SUCCESSFUL. ENTREPRENEURSHIP BEGINS WHEN YOU DECIDE TO INVEST IN YOURSELF AND MAKE THINGS HAPPEN ON YOUR OWN TERMS.

Entrepreneurship does not begin merely when your business is officially established & successful. Entrepreneurship begins when you decide to invest in yourself and make things happen on your own terms.

For example, Google started in a friend's garage. Did anybody know Google then? No, but two students with a vision were working to bring it to fruition.

THAT is entrepreneurship. It is a MINDSET, a mind orientation, of believing & following your own direction.

Building a Business

Building a business does not require a college degree, years of experience, or for you to pass a background, credit, or drug test. It does not require you to sit through 3 interviews, and does not require you to beat out other candidates. Stop thinking it's so hard to build your OWN dreams.

You can waste the rest of your LIFE feeling sorry for yourself and telling anyone who is willing to listen about your sad sob story, that you are broke, struggling, that you get no help, your job sucks or you can't find work, that you are stressed out, sick of having bad credit or you ready to give up and quit life.

OR

You can GET BACK UP, TODAY, start working on your dreams, start fixing your finances, start building your credit, and start your own business so your fate won't be in the hands of others and so that you are able to tell others how you BOUNCED BACK from adversity. Go all out to be successful as you want to be.

Don't act like you're the first person to ever fall down and struggle with drinking problems, drug problems, felonies, sickness, divorce, unemployment, homelessness, foreclosure, car reposession, a negative bank account, or can't find a job.

TRUST me. You are NOT! Turn that PAIN into POWER!!!!!

Now GET UP and go be great!

Being An Entrepreneur Is Hard

Being an entrepreneur is hard, but so is living paycheck to paycheck for 40 years. It's real simple: you either become an entrepreneur, or you work for one. It's easier to start a business than to look and beg for a job.

How Do You Want To Get Paid?

Entrepreneurship is very simple: Either you want to get paid for 8 hours or 24 hours.

People always ask me what are ways to make money online.

• You can develop a fashion or clothing line

• You can train others on financial literacy

• You can drop ship which means you can find products online cheap, mark up the prices then resell it

• You can help others invest in their future (insurance, investments etc)

• You can do coaching sessions on whatever your passion in life is. Makeup, art, beauty, hair etc

• You can do affiliate or network marketing if the product is something people need

• You can sell baked goods or hand crafted items and ship them all over the world

• You can have an online store - it can be beauty products, baby products, health products, toys, games, car parts, the sky is the limit.

• You can use video to give online classes on whatever your gift is - fitness, cooking, making others look good, mentoring etc etc

• You can design websites, logos, help people market, help businesses become computer literate

The sky is the limit. Technology is a gift. Use Instagram, YouTube, Facebook, Twitter, Snapchat and many other sources on the internet to go all out for yours. 6 figures is only $11 an hour 24 hours a day. Entrepreneurs even earn while they sleep.

The Future Is Entrepreneurship

YouTube and Netflix have taken over television programming.

Uber and Lyft have taken over the taxi industry.

Online Shopping (eBay, Amazon etc) has taken over the malls and downsized jobs in the retail & electronic industry.

Streaming services have taken over cable and the movie industry.

Spotify, Apple Music, and Pandora have taken over the music industry (RIP).

AirBNB has taken over the hotel Industry.

• Smartphones have taken over the amateur camera, the digital watch, the mp3 player, handheld gaming consoles, amateur camcorders, GPS maps, the house phone, and the computer industry.

• The internet is building jobs!

I'm saying this because we need to get with the times and keep up. Most people are still 10 years behind the times. Just a few years ago, there wasn't any Uber, Snapchat, AirBnB, Twitter, Instagram, or many of the other things we use every day.

Stop turning your noses up to entrepreneurship opportunities because these jobs are not safe out here. Technology is taking over.

You do know that those secret meetings that the managers and bosses have at your job are about how they can cut costs, how they can replace you for someone that will take lower wages, how they can outsource your work without looking too greedy, and how they can put certain rules in place that will eventually get you fired.

The days of staying at your job long-term is over unless it's a union, in healthcare, if you are in a high level profession or a city, state or government job. Just another reason I teach entrepreneurship.

Think Outside the Box

I genuinely just want people to win. We have to start thinking outside of the box. What worked for our parents isn't going to work for us. That 40 hour work week for 40 years to get 40% when you retire is outdated.

I hate to see all this money out here and we aren't aware of it. There are so many ways to make income we are not aware of. These are secrets they hold from us. If people could stop hating on each other, we could pool our ideas and strengthen each other's weaknesses in an attempt to create generational wealth.

A Million Ways To Make a Million

There are a million ways to make a million dollars with all this education and technology at our finger tips. I see people all over social media helping you build your brand, showing you opportunities, showing you how to become succcesful, and giving you step-by-step directions for the blueprint to success.

You have Twitter, FB, IG, Youtube, and access to a billion consumers. Go get it!

Being skeptical, thinking everything is a scam, not investing in yourself, and keeping too much hate in your heart to build with other people will keep you forever struggling and building other people's dreams.

They taught the elders in your family that working for yourself is laziness, a scam, or a hustle. They taught them hat they would fail, that they would never create wealth, and if they wanted to be safe in life they always had to build other people's dreams. Then your family passed down that same broken mindset to you.

Why do you think almost everybody you know does not support you when you try to build? Why do you think you barely see any people owning businesses? Why do you think when you see social media posts that say someone just got a job, they get hundreds of likes, but when you post up saying that you just started a business, you barely get 1 or 2 likes?

The brainwashing is real. If you are the type who complains, is scared to take chances, or always doubts yourself, don't expect to go very far in life.

So Many Brothers Are Locked Up

Growing up, we were never taught business-building practices or entrepreneurship. Many of us had a real hustler's spirit, but we used it to build drug businesses and have lives of crime.

Had we not looked up to drug dealers growing up and instead looked up to businessmen & women, the drug war that depletes our communities of young men would have been a fail. We only know what we see. Because poor communities have the lowest number of businesses, young men figure the only two ways to get rich are to play ball or sell drugs, but that's false.

Especially with all the technology & information we now have, you can use your hustle spirit to build apps, build businesses, build wealth and build your dream. You can be rich the legal way if you Hustle

SMART, keep a rich mindset, and stop using technology and the internet for dumb stuff. Start using your gifts to become successful.

Because Jobs Don't Pay Enough

$500 if you are lucky to make that much AFTER TAXES x 52 weeks = $26,000

Rent on average $1000 x 12 months = $12,000

Food on average $500 x 12 = $6000

Utilities on average $500 x 12 = $$6000

That ONLY leaves $2000, plus a tax return, to save, have fun, breathe, buy clothes, take care of the kids, get a car, pay for Internet, go away on vacation, pay for a cell phone bill, look good, smell good, and live life.

And you wonder why people are angry and sad, their credit is bad, they have hate in their heart, they are sick, feeling resentful, and struggling so much?

Because these JOBS don't pay enough.

- Your job is paying you 300,400,500 TOPS after taxes for 40-70 hours a week and that is not a scam to you?

- You work every day but you're still broke and that is not a scam to you, either?

- You paid your College 50k - 100k for a piece of paper but can't get a job in that field and, in your mind, you were not scammed at all?

BUT

The moment you are presented with an opportunity to build, create wealth, open your own business, or change your life with something OTHER than building someone else's dream, the 1st thing that comes to the weak mind is that it's a SCAM?

Some of you are on the verge of 3-4 generations under you being broke because of that mindset you have if you do not become Rich-minded and change.

The Entrepreneurship Wealth Formula

The entrepreneur wealth formula is really simple: the work you put in for your own business will pay you for the rest of your life. The work you put in for your job will only pay you next Friday.

Stop giving so much money to Nike, Apple, Samsung, Gucci, the club, the liquor store, and the weed man. Let's use that money and start investing to build. Let's also stop putting so much money in the church if they are not giving back.

If we are to change our collective direction, ownership is the key. Buy some property. Open a business. Get a store front. Support one another.

- Our community needs grocery stores.

- Our community needs cleaners.

- Our community needs gyms.

- Our community needs auto parts stores.

- Our community needs healthy places to eat.

- Our community needs mentoring programs.

Lets get to work!

Why Be An Entrepreneur?

$11.38 a hour as an entrepreneur = $100,000 a year. Entrepreneurs can get paid 24 hours a day, even while sleeping. $11.38 a hour as an employee = $23,640 because they are limited to an 8 hour income.

Do What It takes

So many of us are out there are struggling, feeling down about ourselves, not getting the support we need, or are just financially broken.

Here is some Richminded advice

1.   Do whatever it takes to make all your dreams come true.

2.   Take a few hours everyday to work on reading, researching and building for success.

3.   Stay far away from dream killers and people that have a negative spirit. That includes negativity on social media.

4.   Pray and keep telling yourself you can and will make it.

5.   Whatever is your passion GO FOR IT and don't let anyone or anything stop you. Your worth is determined by your gifts.

Be A Boss

It's easy to get a job, but it takes a real BOSS mentality to provide the jobs!

When you become a boss you can give yourself a raise, a company car, and from your own creativity can take care of your family. You just have to keep pushing, keep grinding, and become an inspiration to others.

Future

YOUR PRESENT CIRCUMSTANCES DON'T DICTATE YOUR FUTURE.

YOU JUST HAVE TO FLY HIGH, FACE THOSE FEARS, AND GO FOR YOURS.

TRUST THE PROCESS, FOLLOW YOUR DREAMS, AND MAKE IT HAPPEN.

Focus On Your Future

Fellas....Pull your pants up, dress the part, stop trying to be a thug and a gangster. Focus on your future, go find a queen, go be great, go build a family, go build wealth, and do something to make others proud.

Saggin' spelled backwards is niggas.

When you walk around like this, you are seen as uneducated bums, idiots, unemployable losers, future convicts, effeminate, immature, no home training, no future, an embarrassment to society, and no father figure. We are better than this.

Your Past Does Not Dictate Your Future

When 50 Cent was a child, he lost his mom when she was allegedly murdered in a house fire. When Tyler Perry was a child, he was physically abused by his father and molested by several adults.

A few years later, 50 Cent sold drugs to survive until he got caught and was sentenced to Prison. A few years later, Tyler Perry became homeless living in abandoned cars.

After he came home from jail, 50 Cent continued dealing in the streets until he was almost murdered. He survived being shot 9 times before Eminem and Dre Dre heard his mixtape and signed him to a deal.

Tyler Perry went after his dreams and did one Comedy Play a year. Every year it would fail, until the seventh year of him trying. Broke and losing faith, he almost gave up and walked away.

50 Cent is a self-made multi-millionaire, has a shoe line, his own record company, has sold millions of records and is executive producer of the highest rated show on Starz called Power.

Tyler Perry now has his OWN studio production company, is worth half a BILLION dollars, has made numerous movies, and employs more

African American actors and actresses than anyone on the planet.

Life is 10% what happens to you, and 90% what you CHOOSE to do about it!!!! Some folks will constantly bring up your PAST, because they are envious and afraid of your FUTURE.

Your Present Circumstances Don't Dictate Your Future, Either

Your present circumstances don't dictate your future. You just have to fly high, face those fears, and go for yours. Trust the process, follow your dreams, and make it happen. Thats all!

Gifts

GOD DID **NOT** PLACE THESE **GIFTS** WITHIN YOU SO THAT YOU COULD SIT AROUND BEGGING FOR THE ACCEPTANCE, AND THE APPROVAL, OF OTHERS.

JUST GET OUT THERE, MAKE POWER MOVES, AND STOP WORRYING ABOUT THESE DREAM KILLERS.

If you cook well, then become a chef. If you are a great with kids, then become a mentor or teacher. If you about business, then teach financial wellness.

If you love pets, open a grooming, dog walking, or pet sitting service. If you love fashion, become a consultant or open a beauty line. If you are good with computers, there are limitless opportunities, If you are great with people and that's your gift, then the sky is the limit!

Just get out there, make power moves, and stop worrying about these dream killers.

No More Excuses

Listen.....

I'm going to make it as simple as I can for you. God gave us all gifts. Each one of us has a unique gift. He didn't give to us so we can play games or stay stagnant. He gave it to us to make moves.

Big moves! As long as we are Richminded, stay humble, focus on success, and help others you will win and be blessed. Everyday use that gift to win.

Use it to open a business. Use it to create wealth. A great routine is to tweet your business on Twitter, post about it on Facebook, put up some pictures on Instagram, and make a video on YouTube. You can easily take 10-20 minutes out of your day to do that and get your business in front of thousands, if not millions, daily. All of that is FREE marketing.

What's the excuse? It doesn't cost a dime to do this daily. It only costs you time.

Also, stop putting a timeline on your success. It may be slow at first, but eventually if you keep pushing, you will blow up.

Stop the fear. Stop holding yourself back from greatness. Stop limiting your worth. Let's go!

Here's a list of excuses...... and my rebuttals

- I can't do that. (Yes, you can.)

- I don't have the money. (Yes, you do. Find it.)

- I don't have the time. (Time is precious, but you have it.)

- I will fail. (No, you won't.)

- I failed already. (So what? Keep pushing!)

- I will end up broke. (You are already almost broke and struggling. What do you have to lose?)

- I'm scared. (Fear stops your greatness.)

- I am not smart enough. (Yes, you are.)

- I have no business experience. (That's nonsense. If you built other people's dreams, you have tons of business experience.)

- It's a scam. (The real scam is spending more hours at work than with your family.)

- I am a minority. (So is Oprah Winfrey, Tyler Perry, and Barack Obama.)

- I am not good enough. (That's because you are Great!)

- I'm afraid of what others might think. (Don't worry about others. I have yet to see any of them put a check in your mailbox.)

Google is free. YouTube is free. Twitter is free. Instagram is free. Snapchat is free. Facebook is free. They haven't shut down, they haven't gone on vacation. They are not too busy.

There is no coupon code required. There's no signup fee. It won't bill you every month, it won't mess up your credit and it won't call your phone asking for money. So why are you sleeping on this type of technology to help make your dreams a reality even when it's FREE?

You can have a million dollars or a million excuses. Choose your million.

Use Your Gifts!

Stop asking other people for permission to use your gifts. STOP worrying what others will think.

If you are a speaker, tell them pass the microphone and SPEAK on it. If you are a writer, then WRITE your butt off. If you are a motivator, then INSPIRE the masses.

If you are a marketer, then MARKET all day, every day. If you have a business, then PROMOTE IT as many times daily as you like. If you are hustling your talent and passion to change your life, then HUSTLE SMART!!!

Others may not like it. Others may not support it, but God did NOT place these GIFTS within you, so that you could sit around begging for the acceptance, and/or the approval of your family & friends and miserable people all over social media. Now go be great and make that money!

Your Gifts Are Worth 6 Figures

If you use your gift to become successful, I promise you will not be struggling financially. I know a chef who made 6 figures last year. I know a handyman who made 6 figures last year. I know multiple barbers and stylists who made 6 figures.

I know many different entrepreneurs that used their gifts and talents to easily make 6 figures. Your gift is not just singing, dancing, or playing ball.

It's whatever you have a passion for doing. We all are good at a lot of things, but each of us is great at something. Use that gift for success.

Goals

W = Write your plans out.

E = Envision your future.

A = Affirm the Talent He gave you.

L = Listen to those who have became successful.

T = Take action & Make moves.

H = Hold your Vision & Hustle SMART.

Bought to you by a R.I.C.H. (Real Intelligent Creative Hustler) mindset.

If you start thinking about real goals and real income, hanging around real go-getters, writing down and visualizing your empire on real paper with a real pen, you better believe your success will get very real for you.

Build Your W.E.A.L.T.H. and Become R.I.C.H.

W = Write your plans out.

E = Envision your future.

A = Affirm the Talent He gave you.

L = Listen to those who have became successful.

T= Take action & Make moves.

H = Hold your Vision & Hustle SMART.

Bought to you by a R.I.C.H. (Real Intelligent Creative Hustler) mindset.

You Need Goals

Without a goal, you will not score. You absolutely need a clear vision or goal (which most people don't have) with definite plans, backed with a definite purpose. Go write a check to yourself or your business for $1,000,000. Postdate it for a year from now. Then, go stick it on the refrigerator.

Every time you are hungry for food, you will see that check and be hungry for success as well. Forget about 5 and 6 figures, let's go for 7. You can do it. Say these 2 letter words to yourself everyday

If it is to be, it is up to me!

From Goal To Got It!

1. See your goal
2. Understand the obstacles
3. Create a positive mentality
4. Clear your mind
5. Embrace the challenge
6. Stay on track
7. Show the world

God

WHAT I FIGURED OUT, WHICH REALLY ENLIGHTENED ME, WAS THAT I HAVE SIMPLY NEVER, EVER SPOKEN TO GOD HIMSELF.

EVERYTHING I KNOW ABOUT HIM, I HAVE LEARNED FROM OTHER HUMANS.

Don't Thank God it's Friday

Thank him for not waking up in a hospital bed, in a jail cell, or being carried in or out of a funeral home, homeless, with bad news, in bad health, or in bad spirits.

Thank him for breathing life today and the ability to go all out for your dreams!

Talk To God About Success

I learned one of my biggest lessons ever in life. I was raised as a Christian because that was all I was exposed to. I occasionally read the Bible. I didn't understand every concept, but I understood a few.

Then, I stopped praying altogether. I grew a lot and I started really studying the Bible and saw what was in it. I discovered how they condoned slavery on many occasions. I read many scriptures about slavery.

Based on what the Bible said, I started to disbelieve in the Christian religion. I realized that one of the reasons it was created was to justify enslaving others. Once I stopped believing in Christianity, my relationship with God suffered. I stopped praying and felt betrayed.

How could God stand for slavery? How could His book of teaching be so foul? Why was so many innocent people being killed all the time? Where was He during slavery? Why did He let all these evil things occur if He created the earth and everything in it? I was confused. I didn't know what to believe.

At times, I even thought He wasn't real. I thought He was just made up to rule and control other humans.

As time went on, I stopped praying consistently. After about 3 years of not praying, I started to realize how much my prayers in the past really meant and how much my life changed for the worse when I stopped praying.

What I didn't realize was, subconsciously, I was speaking my dreams into existence every night with God when I prayed. Doing so had a real effect on my life. When I prayed consistently, my dreams came true.

When I stopped praying, I went through my hardest times.

The reason I'm writing this is in the Richminded book is because I had one of the best and deepest lesson about God I ever had in my life.

The Lesson

First of all, He is real!!! At least, to me, He is. And I'm going to tell you why. What I figured out, which really enlightened me, was that I have simply never, ever spoken to God himself. Everything I know about Him, I have learned from other humans.

I have never, ever spoken to Him personally. I have never, ever heard His TRUTH.

I don't know if He is responsible for building this entire earth. I don't know if He is responsible for all the bad things that happen every day in society. I don't know if He was responsible for slavery. I don't know if He is responsible for all the innocent people that lose their lives every day. I don't know if He is responsible for people dying of starvation.

The FACT is no one knows. No one has spoken to God Himself.

For all we know, God could be this cool, Richminded dude that keeps it real about who He is and what He is responsible for.

I reconnected with God in a deep way and I'm glad I look at things differently. I learned to never assume anything about God. I learned to define Him for myself instead of following any religion created by other humans.

I talk to God every night and I tell Him I love Him, and I'm grateful for the new understanding!

I'm back to praying and talking to God.

This clarity is what I've been looking for, for the past 2 and a half years.

This answers so many of the questions I have been having.

God is my strength. If you are reading this, He is yours too. It doesn't matter if you are religious or not.

What matters is your personal relationship and understanding with him. Define him for yourself. Have a spiritual connection.

But trust.. He is real!!!! In my opinion, at least.

To whoever is reading this section of the Richminded book, I hope you get great value out of it. Know that he got you. Talk to him. Ask questions, and in due time, they will be answered.

No Success Without God

All day yesterday I was thinking about this Bible verse that said commit to the lord and your plans will succeed. To be honest, I didn't know where to find it. So, I picked up the Bible and just opened it up. Boom! I randomly landed on the exact page, looking at the very verse I was searching for.

God must be really trying to tell me something. My plans are not going to exist if He is not involved. That is a lesson for all of us.

Be Blessed, Not Stressed

If you did not wake up in the hospital, jail cell, or the streets there is no need to be in a bad mood, worrying about things that are not in your control, making excuses, or holding grudges. That is all. Be blessed!

If you did wake up in the hospital, jail cell, or the streets, there is no need to be in a bad mood. You are blessed to be alive!

Stop making excuses and find a way to get successful. Stop worrying about how much it cost to invest in yourself. Stop worrying about what will happen if you fail. Stop worrying about what your friends and family are going to think. Stop worrying about your past, and stop worrying about the odds. Just stop worrying, put it in God's hands, and I promise you that you will succeed. But you have to put your foot forward and believe in yourself.

Let's go!

Stop letting negative people in your life tell you "It can't be done" or "It's impossible" or "It will never work." They are actually right, though. It can't be done, it will never work, and it's impossible with THEIR mindset. Keep your mindset positive, and you keep all things possible.

Grow

FROM THIS POINT ON, JUST BE YOURSELF.

POST ABOUT YOUR GOALS & DREAMS AND WHATEVER YOUR PASSION IS DAILY.

PEOPLE SUPPORT OTHERS WHO GIVE VALUE, SO BE A BLESSING TO OTHERS AND OTHERS WILL BE A BLESSING IN WHATEVER YOU DO.

From this point on, just be yourself. Post about your goals and dreams and whatever your passion is daily. People support others who give value, so be a blessing to others and others will be a blessing in whatever you do.

Grow Anyway

As you grow your goals and dream bigger, you will find there are going to be many times that people will give you the side eye. You know, the "Yeah, right. It's going to fail" look.

People who used to rock with you will shy away from you. The closer they are, the farthest they will run. You will get minimal support, if any at all.

They are going to tell you that you CAN'T do it 1000 more times than you CAN do it. They are going to laugh and talk shit behind your back. And there are going to be days where you say "F* IT" and want to give up.

BUT, I promise if you pay these misery loves company people no attention, keep going hard, stop worrying, and let God have your back, you will be surprised at how far you will get in life and how far your dreams can grow.

Health

EVERYDAY.....

WAKE UP
GET IN THE ZONE
GET MOVING
PUT THE RIGHT FOOD IN YOUR BODY
GET READY
GET INSPIRED
GET PERSPECTIVE
DO SOMETHING TO MOVE YOU FORWARD

THAT'S THE RICHMINDED WAY TO START YOUR DAY!

Your mind and body are more connected then you realize.

Understand that it is your duty to keep your body in good health. Otherwise, don't expect to have a strong and clear mind. Your mindset will determine your success.

Make Your Health Your Number One Priority

Your health should always be the number one priority in your life. You can always buy a new home or a new car, but you cannot buy a new body. Your body is irreplaceable, so take care of it!

The Price of Being Broke

Did you know that being broke and constantly struggling directly impacts your emotional state, your self-esteem, your ability to sleep, your libido, your job performance, the happiness of your life, your ability to leave the hood, your ability to find a mate, your energy levels, the rate at which you age, how you interact with people, your ability to do more for your kids, it also leads to sadness, losing hair, lust, hate, envy, and jealousy.

FEAR is causing all of this! You have to stop being AFRAID to make moves and afraid to put yourself out there.

Hustle SMART

Hustle **SMART** to join the **NBA** club: **N**.ever **B**.roke **A**.gain.

The average millionaire has at least **7** different streams of income!

Hustle SMART to join the NBA (Never Broke Again) club. The average millionaire has at least 7 different streams of income!

- Trading

- Sales

- Residual

- Real Estate

- Marketing

- Start-Up

Hustle Online

I would never have thought in a million years that it was possible to make the kind of income that's being made online. I see people buying the cars of their dreams and buying houses that look like mansions. I see people taking first class trips to dream vacations or flying on private jets.

I have personally trained people that are on their way to a million dollars. I see so many ladies blowing it up by putting their all into their gifts and talents and starting their own business to succeed. I see so many dudes that can't get a job due to either not having a college education or having a record that have made a killing online because technology has given them a chance.

Between Instagram, YouTube, Snapchat, Facebook and Twitter, 6 and 7 figures is not out of reach at all. You just have to open your mind that anything is possible and hustle your butt off. Let's get it!

Major Keys to Hustle SMART

- Entrepreneurship

- Branding
- Credit Awareness & Repair
- Saving
- Investments
- Insurance
- Mentorship
- Creating Wealth
- Building Businesses
- Networking
- Helping Families

RICHMINDED Key # 1 Look forward to a bright future.

When you go to bed at night, no matter how your day went, always read, pray, and reflect on the day. Lie down on a positive note, and picture tomorrow's success.

RICHMINDED Key #2 Ask for help when you need it.

I once saw an old man trying to push open a really heavy door, but he couldn't budge it. I stopped to watch his efforts.

Finally, I said to him, "Are you using all your strength?"

"Yes, I am," he said.

I said, "Sir, no, you're not. You were trying to open the door all by yourself. You haven't asked anyone to help you."

Do not let pride prevent your progress. Asking for help is also a strength.

Major Key : To take help from others is also a strength

🔑 RICHMINDED Key # 3 Stop letting money hold you back from your dreams.

The following steps cost $0.00 to pursue your purpose in life.

- Sharing your dreams - $0.00

- Praying to God for guidance - $0.00

- Educating yourself by reading and researching - $0.00

Not having money is just the excuse you let yourself believe is what is holding you back from living the life you want!

Major Key: Don't let money be the excuse not to get up and make your dreams happen.

🔑 RICHMINDED Key # 4 Use social media to build a network of friends.

When you see someone put out a post on social media pertaining to their goals, dreams, aspirations, business whoever likes, shares, comments and supports that person, send them a friend request or follow them.

These are exactly the type of supportive & uplifting people you want in your network to help you build. Follow this same positive pattern as well.

If you see someone on social media posting about their goals, dreams or new business, please support them by saying something inspirational and others will want to follow you too.

It really makes a person's day when they get support. There are too many people hating on each other instead of celebrating each other.

RICHMINDED Key # 5 Stay humble.

Be yourself and be positive. Share your goals, your dreams, ups, downs, low points, high points, and your struggles. Share how much you want to be successful and how successful you want others to be. Be supportive of others and success will flock to you.

Remember: Coins will always make a sound, but paper money is always silent. When your value increases, don't be like those noisy coins. Keep yourself silent and humble. Money talks, but wealth whispers.

RICHMINDED Key # 6 Use your pain to become the best that you can be.

Recently, a young promising player by the name of Jose Fernandez from the MLB team Florida Marlins died in a boating accident. He was well-loved by many. One of his best friends on the team, Dee Gordon, was so distraught at the pre-game ceremony to honor his fallen friend that he wept and struggled to have the energy to play.

But in honor of his friend, and wearing his uniform, he decided to play. He led off the game with a home run. All season long he did not have a single home run as he does not hit for power. As he circled the bases, he cried and broke down, and looked at his friend in the sky.

Major key: Even when you are sad, broken, in pain and struggling, if you bottle up all that energy and use it for the greater good you, too, will have the power to become successful and hit a home run.

🔑 RICHMINDED Key # 7 Use your talent to create a job

I came across a recently laid-off young man that makes about $300 a day with his grill cooking and selling BBQ chicken, burgers, and shrimp kabobs. He told me his passion was cooking and that he loved grilling.

He told me he couldn't find a job so he went and created one. This is a great example for using your gift to succeed. Use your passion and open a business. Here is a quick list of businesses that you can start right now:

- Business Consultant
- Event Planner
- Become an Author
- Open a Clothing Line
- Food Delivery Service
- Event DJ, Personal Trainer
- Tax Preparer
- Home Improvement
- Auto Broker
- Graphic Design
- Computer Repair
- Household Services (lawn, carpet cleaning, maid)
- Hairstylist
- Open a Barber Shop

- Open a Restaurant or Food Truck
- Juice Bar
- Give Music or Dance Lessons
- Small Business Marketing
- Photography
- Real Estate & Flipping Houses
- Buying and reselling on eBay
- Day Care
- Pet sitting
- Open a travel agency
- Auto detailing
- Baking
- Cleaning services for businesses
- Handyman services
- Open a hiring agency
- Catering
- Senior citizen assistance
- Tutoring
- Become a business or life coach
- Website Design

 RICHMINDED Key # 8 Stop trying to

make small minded people believe in your BIG vision.

Do not associate yourself with negative, unsupportive, ignorant, skeptical, jealous, scared to go after success, scared to invest in themselves, always gossiping, always hating, always blaming others for their failures, backstabbing, insecure, judgmental, lazy, narcissistic, limited thinkers. This will hold you back from greatness.

 *RICHMINDED Key # 9 Use the RICH-MINDED math formula for success.*

ADD people who support you, SUBTRACT your haters, MULTIPLY your greatness, and DIVIDE up your profits.

 *RICHMINDED Key # 10 Stop worrying what others might think of you.*

If you ever feel uneasy about sharing your dreams and goals or your business plans because of offending family or friends, here's a test. When your mailman comes to your mailbox today with a handful of bills, see how many come in your family and friend's name.

 *RICHMINDED Key # 11 Stop waiting, because time is our most precious commodity.*

Stop waiting:

- until you finish school, until you go back to school
- until you get your taxes, until you get a raise

- until you lose ten pounds, until you gain ten pounds
- until you have kids, until your kids leave the house
- until you start working, until you retire
- until you get married, until you get divorced
- until you speak with your husband , until you speak with your wife
- until you get paid this Friday, until you get paid next Friday
- until you get a new car or home, until your car or home is paid off
- until spring, until summer, until fall … until winter
- until you've had a drink, until you've sobered up
- until you die, until you are born again

to decide to go after your dreams and GO HARD for success.

⚷ *RICHMINDED Key # 12 Use your gifts to get money the legal way.*

If you are out there doing illegal criminal activities to produce income that will potentially get you locked up, stop it. There are much better and safer ways to earn. Take away those criminal thoughts and turn them into becoming a successful entrepreneur.

Most of us were never taught how to open a business, how to manage legit money, how to combine our street smarts with our book smarts for success, or how to create wealth other than working for someone or illegal activities.

Use your gift, use technology, and use your hustle mentality to research everything about business. You can find all the information you need on the internet. You do not want to be locked up away from your families, working for slave wages, and begging people to send you commissary money. Jail is not the place to be.

RICHMINDED Key # 13 Understand the value of time.

To realize the value of One Year, ask a solider who hasn't been home in 365 days.

To realize the value of One Month, ask a mother who gave birth to a premature baby.

To realize the value of One Week, ask the editor of a weekly newspaper.

To realize the value of One Day, ask the person who was born on February 29th.

To realize the value of One Hour, ask the lovers who are waiting to meet.

To realize the value of One Minute, ask a person who missed the bus or train.

To realize the value of One Second, ask a person who just avoided an accident.

To realize the value of One Millisecond, ask a person who won a silver medal in the Olympics.

RICHMINDED Key # 14 Keep your circle nice and tight.

You don't need a lot of friends. You need only a good few friends that will up support you, help uplift you, not judge you, not prey your downfall, have your same mindset and hold you down.

RICHMINDED Key # 15 Use technology to your advantage.

If you bought a smartphone, tablet, or computer and have not attempted to make money with any of these devices, you are hustling backwards.

Use this amazing technology. You have to push for your dreams and make income for yourself.

RICHMINDED Key # 16 Pray.

Pray and ask God to help you build on the talent he gave you. Talk to him like you talk to your friends. There is no shame in praying and asking for help on what you want to do.

Also, open your mouth and network. Network = Net Worth. Use your eyes so you can wake up, have vision, and see the greatness coming to you. Don't just use them to watch other people's successes. Use them for your advantage.

Use your hands to build. Build your empire. Build your greatness. You have a gift, use it. He gave you two feet for a reason.

Take action and walk in your purpose. Get moving. You will struggle standing still.

RICHMINDED Key # 17 Your why has to be big enough.

A few years ago there was a runner in the Olympic Games by the name of Derrick Redmond. As he was racing on the track, his dreams as a sprinter were crushed when, all of a sudden, a hamstring injury took him out of the race. Instead of giving up and admitting he was defeated, giving over to the pain and quitting like many others would have done in that same position, he was determined to cross the finish line.

Hobbling towards the end of the race, he is almost overcome by the pain, but his Dad burst onto the track and helped him make it to the finish line. Your WHY has to be big enough to get you to the next level.

Major key: Sometimes you need to support and uplift people to cross that finish line. Your why has to be so strong that you cross the finish line and complete your vision even if you are in a lot of pain, and never give up.

RICHMINDED Key # 18 Every gift you have is a stream of income.

If you can cook, that's a stream of income. If you have the gift of selling, that's a stream of income. If you like kids, that's a stream of income. If you like helping people financially, that's a stream of income. If you like helping people look good, that's a stream of income.

A job is a form of income, but it's not the only way you can make income. The greater the gifting, the bigger the stream.

RICHMINDED Key # 19 Take care of your health.

It's not just colds, the flu, viruses and diseases that make you sick. Being broke all the time makes you sick. Bad credit makes you sick. Being stuck around negative people will make you sick. Unhealthy relationships make you sick. Being underpaid and overworked makes you sick.

Not getting support from your family & friends will make you sick. The unhealthy negative content on your social media accounts that you see daily will make you sick. Seeing other people succeed while you are unsuccessful will make you sick. What you read in the media will make you sick. People who kill your dreams will make you sick.

These jobs will definitely make you sick. Being stuck will make you sick. You have to watch out what you feed yourself, and I'm not just talking about food.

RICHMINDED Key# 20 Become the opposite of all things negative.

Ignorance has 9 letters, but so does Knowledge.

Negative has 8 letters, but so does Positive.

Failure has 7 letters, but so does Success.

Below has 5 letters, but so does Above.

Lying has 5 letters, but so does Truth.

Poor has 4 letters, but so does Rich.

Fail has 4 letters, but so does Pass.

Hate has 4 letters, but so does Love

RICHMINDED Key # 21 Don't let fear stop your greatness.

You are stressed out. You are overworked. You are underpaid. You only have a few dollars in the bank. You can't sleep. You're not eating right. When you do get sleep, you dread waking up to face the day.

Your credit is bad because you misused it because you didn't make enough money.

You are in a lot of debt. You are working just to pay bills. You have no savings, you can't get a loan, and you have nowhere to turn. Your looks are fading because you worry all the time. Your personality is taking a turn for the worse because you are so miserable from finances.

Do you know why this happens?

- Because of a lack of vision.

- Because you turn away and ignore opportunities to win.

- Because you don't believe in yourself.

- Because you are so programmed that you won't even try anything outside your comfort zone.

You think building other people's dreams is more important than building your own.

You believe others when they tell you that you can't have a nice house, or nice car, or your own business, or be successful based on your name, skin color, where you're from, or your past.

You settle for less

You spend so much time watching other people win instead of using that time to build your future.

You get caught up in everything the media says or portrays and you take your focus off you becoming great.

You stay in the same place your whole life.

You have to travel and go where your heart is, where the money is at, where opportunity lives. Fear is what is holding you back from success. Do not let fear stop you.

RICHMINDED Key # 22 Strangers are your real supporters.

Your family & close friends will not support you until strangers do and then when you become successful, they turn around and ask you, "Why are you treating me like a stranger?!"

Don't get caught up in looking for support in family and people who have known you a long time. Just get out there and hustle hard in front of 7 billion people.

RICHMINDED Key # 23 Use the internet to become profitable.

Start a blog and publish everything. Start an Instagram account and post pictures about your business. Start a YouTube channel.

Talk about everything that you are passionate about in your channel. Life advice, makeup, sports, fashion, trends, music, dating, cooking. The sky is the limit. Talk about everything. Do not limit your topics. Sell something and profit. Clothing, shoes, coaching, or whatever your passion is in life!

RICHMINDED Key #24 Become successful or work for someone who is.

Go hard to become successful or spend the rest of your life working hard for someone who does.

RICHMINDED Key # 25 Success matters.

Not only do lives matter, but supporting each other matters, building up our communities matters, teaching our kids respect and manners matters, not killing each other matters, keeping our men out the system matters, building businesses matters, not having so many broken homes for our children matters, getting ourselves out of poverty matters, and repairing broken mindsets matters.

RICHMINDED Key # 26 Skyrocket your success.

Get your mind right, your bank account right and your focus for the future in order and I promise life will be good and your success will skyrocket.

 RICHMINDED Key # 27 Before you give your heart to someone, make sure they have your back.

1. They will support you and not belittle your dreams or the struggle to become successful.

2. They are ready to take on the world with you.

5. They have great expectations, plan to build a family, and will go all out to hustle with you, uplift you, and help take you both towards greatness.

6. Their personality matches or outshines their looks.

Major key: There are billions of people out there so don't settle! On your path to success you will need the right person in your corner.

RICHMINDED Key # 28 Never let your past dictate your future.

Just believe in yourself, focus on your goals, stop procrastinating and keep pushing towards success. Don't let any of these dream killers stop you.

 # RICHMINDED Key # 29 Hustle SMART to never be broke.

Being broke turns into bad credit, living in the hood, turning to crime, getting incarcerated, homelessness, and goverment assistance, It leads to problems in our family structure, turning to drugs, becoming an alcoholic, depression, anxiety, anger, sadness, loneliness, jealousy, envy, and hate. We have to go all out using our purpose, talents, and gifts to never, ever worry about income.

The stress and worry is so HIGH because the level of hustle is so LOW. Get off your butt if you plan to be rich!! You have a mouth, eyes, ears, hands and feet for a reason. Put as much passion into building your own dreams as you did building others.

 # RICHMINDED Key # 30 Go all out creating your own dreams.

Put as much passion into building your own dreams as you did perfecting your resume, faxing your resume to 100 companies, waiting by the phone with all the patience in the world for a job to call you, going to multiple interviews, changing your personality up to impress the interviewers, and spending any amount of money to dress to impress.

If you go all out for creating your own dreams as you do for getting a paycheck that pays you much less than you are worth, success will be right around the corner.

 # RICHMINDED Key #31 Stop hating on

each other.

Sky's the limit if we stop hating on each other, mean mugging one another, watching each other's pockets, and start networking with each other, supporting one another, and picking each other's brains to build empires.

Instead of hating on each, copying each other, competing with each other and recruiting each other to build someone else's dream, I hope we can start building together, investing together, putting our thoughts together and start collaborating to build our net worth. The more you hate on people, the less your income becomes. Always remember that.

Plenty of money to be made out here if we really start supporting each other and stop making other people rich. That's my focus. If this is your focus as well, let's get together and build.

 ## RICHMINDED Key # 32 Losers Compete. Winners Collaborate.

Working together is how you win. Your Network helps grow your Net Worth

We were not taught to think for ourselves or create jobs or become rich. So, I will provide you with keys on how to get your people to support your vision and build together:

1. Be yourself. Stop faking success. If you are struggling, tell the world your pain. People can tell when you are fake balling.

2. Reach out personally through social media or phone and have a conversation on what exactly your vision is.

3. Ask your people questions on their financial situations and how you can collaborate so both of you can build. Closed mouths don't get fed.

4. Most people don't know how to support you. Teach them what support is and lead by example.

5. Let people know you are there for them. You should always stay open for help. God likes helpers. He blesses them.

6. People are struggling so hard and don't know anything about making money. Money will come. Just network, build, be humble, and hustle SMART.

7. Explain how creating jobs and building businesses can create jobs, build our communities, help us come up and build wealth for our families. Most do not know this.

RICHMINDED Key # 33 Use your heart and help others.

You are going to keep struggling, living paycheck to paycheck, and no doors will open up for you UNLESS you use your heart and try and help others, support others to win, help mentor people in need, take action, stop worrying, and have faith in Him. Stop the hating and jealousy, stop watching other people's pockets, start paying yourself first, believe in yourself, and stop wasting valuable time with your life.

RICHMINDED Key # 34 Time is of the essence.

Life is too short for you to be getting paid below your worth, for you to be living paycheck to paycheck, for you to be scared to make moves, for you to be stuck in mediocrity, for you to always have bad credit, for you to be working so hard and still barely have enough to do the things you want to do in life, to be always be worrying and looking over your shoulder, not knowing if your job is going to fire you or lay you off. Life is absolutely way too short for you to be struggling so much. Time to go all out for success.

RICHMINDED Key # 35 Stay away from loser mentalities.

Do not associate yourself with negative, unsupportive, brokeminded, ignorant, dreamkilling, skeptical, jealous, scared to go after success, scared to invest in themselves, always gossiping, always worshiping celebs, always hating, always blaming others for their failues, back-stabbing, closeminded, insecure, judgemental, nogetter, lazy, narcisstic, limited thinkers. You deserve much better people in your circle.

RICHMINDED Key # 36 Make sure you have real people that have your back in your circle.

We all have to support each other when needed, no questions asked.

You - I need $100

Fake Friends/Family - WHY?

You - I need $100

Real Friends/Family - No problem. I've got you covered.

RICHMINDED Key # 37 Always have multiple streams of income.

Did you know that with only 1 income, if you pay an average mortgage or average rent, have a small car note, pay electric, gas, water, cell bill, cable/Internet, and insurance that's about on average $2400 monthly ($600 week)

That does not include food, savings, gas, entertainment, kids, health products, fashion, and other expenses.

If you do not make at least $600 every week AFTER taxes, you are working basically to breath air and pay bills.

There is no law that says because you have a 9-5 you can't make extra income. You will NEVER be broke if you Hustle SMART and have multiple streams of income.

RICHMINDED Key # 38 Talk to God about success.

Pray and ask him what your gift is and, also, ask to become successful. You have to ask.

He needs to know you are committed to yourself, committed to him, committed to helping others, and committed to your business.

RICHMINDED Key # 39 Never stop grinding! Your breakthrough is coming.

There are going to many times you want to give up, quit on yourself, and say, "The hell with going after success." But you have to keep pushing, keep praying, and keep going. Your delay is not your denial. It's coming sooner than you think.

RICHMINDED Key # 40 Stop complaining.

If you complain about being broke daily, weekly, monthly, or yearly, and you ignore opportunities for success, then it's all on you. There is NO excuse not to get it.

There are a million ways to make a million dollars with all this education and technology at our finger tips on ways to become financially free and open a business.

What I find is that most people are just too lazy to learn, scared to death to invest in themselves, programmed to believe that the only way to make an income is through a 9-5, and most importantly, have no belief in their ability to prosper.

We have to change our mindsets. We can all win if we stop b.s.'ing and start envisioning success.

 *RICHMINDED Key # 41 Do not let racism into your life. Everybody is not racist.*

We are all human and it's all love. It's not about white vs. black. It's about no-getters vs. go-getters. It's about people who are trying to support each other and uplift each other vs. people who don't give a damn about you.

We all want the best for our families and all want to live the good life. People who are racist try to divide us, but we are too smart to let it stop us all from becoming successful.

RICHMINDED Key # 42 Some will. Some won't. So what?

Keep it moving. There are 7 billion people on this earth. Trust me, somebody out there is going to support you, help you rise, hold you accountable, and help you build your dreams. And if you can't find any one, I'm right here for you.

RICHMINDED Key # 43 Stop being comfortable and become tired.

If you are going to become successful, you have to first become TIRED.

- Tired of being broke.

- Tired of living paycheck to paycheck.

- Tired of just making it.

- Tired of other people wanting to see you fail.

- Tired of the rat race.

- Tired of giving away too much of your time.

- Tired of all the b.s. that's keeping you struggling.

- Tired of people and their brokeminded opinions.

The list goes on and on. You have to stop being so comfortable and become tired of the madness.

When you are comfortable, you will be either be broke or a paycheck or two away from being broke.

When you are tired of the games, tired of working just to pay bills, tired of your job, tired of not having nice things, tired of living in the hood, tired of struggling, tired of living check to check, and tired of not getting paid what you deserve, then and only then will you start making changes to go after success.

Once you become tired of the madness, you will do whatever it takes to succeed.

RICHMINDED Key # 45 Save money.

Cut back on a few things and put aside at least $27 every day for the next 365 days. In a year, you will have saved $10,000. Use that money to build your dreams. If you are focused and believe in yourself that $10,000 could turn into Millions.

I have a few people I know who turned 10k into wealth. My greatest study material for Hustle SMART was a book called The Richest Man in Babylon. I learned 7 important Major Keys from this book.

1. Pay Yourself First

2. Live below your means

3. Make your money work for you.

4. Insurance protects your wealth.

5. Have a retirement plan.

6. Invest in yourself.

7. Track your wealth.

RICHMINDED Key # 46 Let your haters become your motivators.

When you think of giving up, slacking off, being scared to make moves, quitting, not giving yourself a chance, procrastinating on your goals and dreams, worrying you will fail or fearful that your success won't work please think of all the haters around you that want to see you fail, all the people who slept on you, all the people who paid you way below your worth and all the people who tried to kill your dreams. Let the haters become your motivaters.

RICHMINDED Key # 47 We all have gifts – use THEM!

We all have a gift, talent, and passion for something. Many of us like to write, dance, teach, help others, sing, make others look good (barber,makeup,hair,fashion), coach, love pets, like to work with kids, are artistic, love to work on homes, love cars, love computers, love movies, love to travel, love sports. You can turn whatever you love doing into income.

Your boss did it. The founders of the social media sites you frequent did it. The makers of the clothes you are wearing did it. Your barber or salon person that have you looking good did it. Everything that you love to do has an entrepreneur behind it that did it with their gift, passion, love, and talent and SO CAN YOU.

My point is we all have greatness inside us. Use it to earn, Use it to better your situation, Use it for a better less stressful life. Stop giving all your time to everyone else and start doing you. 2 ways will lead you into your fate...Inspiration or Desperation.

RICHMINDED Key # 48 Shock the world.

Recently, while viewing the NBA Finals, something impossible happened. LeBron James and the Cleveland Cavs upset and shocked the world. But this is bigger than basketball. People hated on Lebron James, wrote his team off, and didn't give them a chance in the world after being down 3-1 to the Golden State Warriors.

Right now YOU are down 3-1. People will hate on you, not give you a chance in hell at success, and will write you off like you are washed up and DONE. They will even tell you that you cannot win and you will fail and you will never be anything. That's just how most people roll. They want you just as miserable as they are.

But you have to face the fear, beat the odds, and pull from within to show everybody you are a winner and you will never ever give up trying to win. People are watching your every move, waiting for you to fail and waiting for you to lose, but you are much better than that. I want you to pull off an upset and shock the world as well by going all out for your dreams, becoming successful, and never ever giving up.

RICHMINDED Key # 49 BURN

Sometimes you have to BURN up a friendship or BURN some bridges to let people know you on FIRE!

RICHMINDED Key # 50 Dreams don't work unless you do.

A friend of mine was sick and tired of being broke. So he saved up 25k by not blowing money on b.s., limiting HIS nightlife, not buying materialistic items, and being focused on his dreams. He took the 25k and went and got his dealer license, rented an $800 trailer, went to the auto auction, and bought 10 cars.

He opened a buy here, pay here, no credit check dealership. Those 10 cars bought him in over 4k a month profit and that enabled him to keep buying more cars. Now he makes over 15k monthly profit, is about to open a 2ND dealership, has employees, and is now winning big. Nothing is going to work if you not ready to put in hard work and hustle.

RICHMINDED Key # 51 Be thankful.

Be thankful for the love, the hate, the support, the non-support, the highs, the lows, the lessons, the blessings, the setbacks, the comebacks, when they celebrate you and when they damn sure underestimate you. Be thankful for it all, because that is how you win.

RICHMINDED Key # 52 Never take advice from somewhere not going anywhere in life.

CLOSED minded people always got their mouths OPEN saying what you can and can't do.

RICHMINDED Key # 53 Small moves

turn into medium moves.

Make a few small moves that turn into medium moves and then you will be in position to make a very big move.

 ## *RICHMINDED Key # 54 See the world.*

Get up, get out, travel, look on realtor.com or apartments.com. Look for jobs in other cities or build a business from home and work anywhere on earth. Change your surroundings, change your circle, and get away from the negative people and the no-getters.

It's a big world out there with plenty of money in it. Go get yours. Your blessings might be right around the corner but, unfortunately, some of you never leave the block. People act like the only place to live is where they grew up. Go explore the world.

 ## *RICHMINDED Key # 55 Believe in yourself.*

Always believe in yourself and success will follow you.

Invest

DON'T BE A D.U.M.B.A.S.S.!

D.ON'T
U.NDERSTAND
M.ONEY
B.UT
A.LWAYS
S.AYING
S.CAM

BE R.I.C.H.MINDED
(REAL INTELLIGENT CREATIVE HUSTLER!)

Know your worth. Investing in yourself pays the highest returns!

Richminded Business Plan for Success:

- Invest in the following:
- Personal Growth
- Seminars/Training to Build your Mindset
- Traveling to Network with Mentors
- Your Health
- Your Dreams
- Starting a Business
- Investments that grow money
- Pray Often
- Take Action
- More Reading and Less TV
- Use Technology to reach millions
- Build with likeminded Individuals
- Don't walk, but run, after Success

The World Is Yours! Go get it

Don't Be a D.U.M.B.A.S.S.

Don't be a D.U.M.B.A.S.S (D.on't U.nderstand M.oney B.ut A.lways S.aying S.cam) Becoming an entrepreneur and working for yourself is not a scam. Let me tell you what a real scam is: Let me drop a secret that they never shared with you. You are getting paid for 40 hours, but it's actually 100 hours a week you are giving away to your job. (20 hours a day)

6am-7am - Get ready for work

7am-8am - Transportation to work

8am-5pm - Work

5pm-6pm - Transportation home from work

6pm-10pm - Freedom

10pm - 6am - 8 hours sleep to function at work

Now divide your pay by 100 hours and that's what you are actually paid every week for your time. That's a real scam!

Don't be a D.U.M.B.A.S.S., Part 2

Becoming an entrepreneur and working for yourself is not a scam but let me tell you what a real scam is:

• Claiming other people's kids during tax time.

• Selling foodstamps for cash.

• Having your working man live with you in that section 8 apartment.

• Prostituting yourself .

• Boosting.

• Selling drugs.

• Lying to get disability.

• Student loans.

- Rent-a-center & Rent-a-rims.

- Payday loans.

- Anything else to prevent us from winning or putting us in the system.

The point is: don't let ignorance prevent you from progressing to do some big things. Building wealth is not a scam.

Don't Be a D.U.M.B.A.S.S, Part 3

FYI: you cannot do GREAT things with d.u.m.b.a.s.s. people.

Don't Be a D.U.M.B.A.S.S., Part 4

Why is it when the new iPhone drops, you have $300, $400, $500, or $600 ready? When the new Jordans drop, you stand in line for hours and are ready to drop $200, $300, or $400? When you need some hair, you are ready to drop $200, $300, or $400 on the best Brazilian bundles. When you want to buy Red Bottoms or a Gucci Bag, money is no object.

On the weekend, you go out and spend $200, $300, $400, or $500 in the club to impress people with not a care in the world. You even spend money endlessly to impress others with your fake success for likes on social media, knowing you are struggling.

But when it's time to invest in yourselves to makes moves to better your situation it's always, "I don't have any money. I'm broke right now. I'm low on cash. I'm waiting on next month." Excuse after excuse. You are lying to yourself. You are not broke.

You are just scared because you think you will fail. You have no faith in yourself to win. You have it for material items all the time but you don't value yourself enough to invest in yourself. Think about that! You don't even see the value in yourself to spend on YOU!

That mindset has to change. I'm telling you, if you focus on your dreams and invest in yourself to become successful, you can have whatever you want in life. Just create the vision that makes you want to jump out the bed in the morning, and I promise you will succeed.

Let me tell you why people will always live check 2 check and always be at the mercy of others. Because they let fear steal their hope. Because they are afraid of opportunity, and because they do not believe in themselves.

Fear is the greatest trick the devil ever pulled. Fear will keep your bank accounts very low. Fear will keep you with a bum mentality. Fear will keep you driving an old car with 200k miles on it. Fear will keep you in the hood. Fear will keep you paying high rent with nothing to show for it.

Fear will keep you with bad credit. Fear will keep you dancing at work, not knowing at any minute that they are looking to cut back and replace you. Fear will keep you lying to yourself, saying you want to be successful, but not doing a damn thing to make moves.

Fear will keep you looking at others success and eventually make you jealous, bitter, and a hater. Why do you think 95% of people on your friends list don't support you?

It's because they are scared to be great, too! You have to wake up and stop making excuses to become successful because fear is killing you slowly.

I Am Looking For People!

I want to work with people who want to open their own brand.

Qualifications are

- You are ready to make 6 and 7 figures.

- You are ready to lift your talents and gift to become successful.

- You are ready to make financial changes so you can stop the madness of limited income.

- You are ready to invest in yourself to make major moves.

- You are ready to finally see a light at the end of the tunnel and stop following everybody's dreams and put your own into action.

The procrastinating stops today.

The only way you are going to be successful is if you stop listening and trying to get validation from brokeminded people, focus on your gift, do what YOU love to do, stop following what others are doing, put all your heart into it, and trust God that it will be great. It will all fall into place. You will see!

Life

FAKE PEOPLE HAVE AN IMAGE TO MAINTAIN.

REAL PEOPLE JUST DO WHAT MAKES THEM HAPPY. THEY ARE REALLY NOT CONCERNED WITH THE OPINIONS OF OTHERS.

How much longer will you continue to live this way? How much longer will you settle for a life that you HATE Monday-Thursday, prior to thanking God for Friday?

How much longer will you settle for showing up to a job that you hate, doing work that you hate, with people that you hate?

At what point will YOU take control? At what point will YOU demand better? At what point will you come to realize that YOU have the power to CHANGE all of this?

As my favorite song from Outkast would say - You better GET UP, GET OUT, and DO something! Don't let the days of your life pass you BY!!!!

Everything You Do Isn't Everybody's Business

We don't have to put everything we buy, every accomplishment, everywhere we go, every time we are at the hospital, every time we get into a new relationship, every time we get a new job, every drama we ever face, every time we get a new cell phone, Jordan's, hairstyle, clothes or every time we out at the club on social media for likes.

Everything you do isn't everybody's business. Use some of that energy to build and change your circumstances. Likes = $0.00

Watch the Company You Keep

My favorite rapper, and someone I used to look up to, wanted to be a revolutionary and change the world. He had the charisma, the passion, and the fire to do it. He could cut you down with his words.

He actually used to go hood to hood and ask the dealers to stop dealing. They respected him so much that they would stop. He started a Thug Life lifestyle, but in a good way. He created a way to clean brothers up and clean up the community.

Then, he got involved with the wrong people. He started hanging with low lives that thought banging was cool. He started listening to dream killers who told him that it was cool to want to kill another brother and stop all that revolutionary garbage. He listened to them, started acting like a wanna-be gangbanger, and next thing you know, he lost his life. His name was Tupac Shakur.

Moral of my story: Watch the company you keep. Watch out for dream killers & no-getters because they will steal your dreams and put you in a position to lose everything including your life.

Stop supporting:

• Liquors stores in your community

• Payday loans and check cashing stores (Grow up and use a bank or credit union)

• Rental Centers

• Asian Hair Care Stores

• Nasty Fried Chicken Stores

• Nasty Chinese Restaurants

• Any store that sells unhealthy food

• Places that sell cheap jewelry

• Sneaker stores in the hood

• Title Loan companies that rip off the poor

• These death trap hood nightclubs

• Any business that has bulletproof glass in it.

These businesses are there to take from you, prey on you, make you unhealthy, and keep you in the struggle. These owners do not respect you, don't want to hire you, and their bottom line is to make money off you. Open your eyes.

Nicki or Ayesha?

Ask your daughter who Nicki Minaj is. Now ask your daughter who Ayesha Curry is.. There is a 99% chance that she will only be able to tell you who Nicki is.

Allow me to explain: Nicki is a rapper who teaches your daughter how to be a hoe, teaches her to show her body to the world with no consequences, glorifies butt injections and self-destruction of the body. She has become a toxic teacher of young girls and a role model from hell.

In Nicki's world, a young girl should never waste time with a man who might be a good husband and father. Instead, according to her lyrics, girls should be chasing dope boys, "killaz", and baby daddies.

Ayesha Curry is the wife of basketball phenom Steph Curry. She is also a mother of two, a paid speaker, an author of two books, has her own food delivery company, and is on her way to becoming the next Martha Stewart. Her highly rated cooking show was just picked up for a second season on the Food Network. She also mentors young girls on entrepreneurship, family values, and becoming successful in life. She motivates her husband to be the best that he can be. Even though her husband has millions of dollars, that did not stop her hustle or her desire to give back.

Your daughter has barely HEARD of role models such as Ayesha Curry, whose success can show her how to act like a lady. Instead, she tries to emulate what she thinks will validate her as a woman by following people like Nicki Minaj who make her think tons of makeup, different color weaves, having a fat butt, and chasing after anacondas are the way to make her feel good and keep her esteem high.

The system and media pushes people like Nicki, and countless others, onto the mind and spirit of our young princesses so they can think things like stripping, selling or showing their body, being a baby momma, and sleeping with many men is cool.

Help teach our young girls better. Help them realize the power they hold and help them believe in themselves that they rock and they are all beautiful and I promise you will have a very special girl that will grow into a wonderful woman.

Future or Maverick?

Ask your son about Future. Now ask your son about Maverick Carter. There is a 99% chance that your son will only be able to tell you about Future.

Allow me to explain: Future is a rapper who teaches your son to trap and deal in drugs, teaches him to pop Molly and Percocet's, teaches your son that it is cool to f"ck up some commas, call women freak hoes, and to shoot and kill other brothers. His music, and so many other mainstream rap artist lyrics, are definitely part of the problem keeping us entrapped and enslaved in the system.

Maverick Carter is Lebron James's business manager. He's worth millions of dollars. He negotiated Lebron's $1 billion-plus lifetime deal with Nike and helped put Beats Music on the map. He just played a central role in the largest celebrity apparel deal of all time and turned a young black ballplayer from Akron into a billion-dollar global brand.

Despite being a YOUNG BROTHER that grew up poor he can get negotiate, make deals, and make things happen more than most high-level business people on the planet.

The lesson here: your son can make millions not just from being an athlete or rapper, but also by being an entrepreneur or BEAST in the boardroom.

Your son has never even HEARD of Maverick Carter whose success can show him how to have a very bright future. Instead, he idolizes, emulates, and dreams of becoming the rapper called Future.

That right there is definitely is a past, present, and (no pun intended) FUTURE problem!!!

Don't Feed the Prisons

The prison system is a business. They make well over $100 a day if we are locked up. Believe me, they want us locked up and the key thrown away. They barely want us to have a good job and to support our families out here in these streets. So many of us turn to doing whatever we can to survive.

Trust and believe whatever nonsense you are doing out there is going to lead to 3 things: death, prison, or having a record that will keep you from ever getting a good job, no matter what people say.

I implore you to look into your heart and use that hustle to build your own dream. Look into becoming an entrepreneur and help out other brothers and sisters in your same struggle. Use your gift and talent to do big things. Don't use it to end up a statistic.

Be Real

You would be amazed to know the number of folks who make every decision in life based upon the desire to impress OTHERS.

What will people think if I buy this car?

What will people think if I buy this house?

What will people think if I buy these shoes?

What will people think if I work this job?

What will people think if I date this guy/girl?

FAKE people have an IMAGE to maintain. REAL people just do what makes THEM happy. They are really not concerned with the opinions of others.

There Are No Perfect Men

For the single ladies out there... There is no such thing as a perfect man. Just find someone that you want to build with, someone that has a great mindset, a good heart, and makes you happy. Who are you trying to find out here in these streets... GOD?

Stop!

Stop waiting!

Strangers will support you more than family and friends ever will. Use your gift to get money the legal way. Use technology to push your dreams and make an income for yourself. Use your passion and open a business.

You know why strangers support you more than people you actually know? Because the people you know have a tough time accepting that you come from the same place, but they're still stuck there.

Impossible is a lie. If you want it, go and get it. Use the internet to become profitable. Sell something and profit. Clothing, Shoes, Coaching, or whatever your passion is in life!

Stop hating on other people's success.

Are you going to sit around for the rest of your LIFE telling everybody the sad story about how you did time and caught a felony? Or are you going to start writing the NEXT chapter? What defines us is how we rise AFTER falling down. It is okay to fall down, Just don't unpack and STAY down there!!!!!! GO GET IT!!

Stop worrying about the thoughts of others.

Stop letting people SLEEPING on you....deter you from your DREAMS. To get to where you are going, you have drop some people off first! It's simple math. Add go-getters, subtract haters, divide profits, multiply your greatness. Stop worrying about what your friends and family are going to think.

If you have a million dollar vision pleeeeeeeaaaassse stop surrounding yourselves and listening to people who have a 1 cent mindset and start making moves to build your empire. 90% of your happiness or misery in life depends on who you choose to spend it with, so choose very carefully. People with nothing to do will never understand what you are trying to get done.

Stop letting FEAR stop you from becoming great! Scared = BROKE.

Simple Math.... A OUNCE of action will always overcome a TON of fear. The more action you take and moves you make, the more you go to the bank. Don't let FEAR stop you.

Stop calling yourself a small business owner....Think BIG!

For the Ladies and the Fellas

Ladies....make sure he has goals, ambitions, wants to build a family, wants success, wants out the hood and wants to go all out to give you the world. If not, there are plenty of brothers out there that are about that life.

Fellas....She doesn't want just a gift to make her happy. She wants you to get some hustle, change your mindset, start creating wealth for the future, and to become a go-getter and handle business for your family. That would be a very great gift for her.

Get Out

Ladies:

- From any toxic relationship. You are beautiful, you are a queen, and you deserve the best. If he not trying to build a family with you, wife you up, and do big things with you, then move on.

- From this stigma that likes on social media give you validation. You don't have to keep putting up pic after pic showing your body to get attention. You are not Kim K or Nicki Minaj. These celebs got you thinking this is normal to show your butt to thousands of thirsty people on social media when it is not. Show some class and act like a lady. That's how you get taken seriously.

- From the Struggle. Use your gifts to make a come up. You are the fastest rising entrepreneurs in the world. Use your talents to create fashion, beauty, coaching, and businesses that will change the world. Especially for the single mothers. Don't let that excuse hypnotize you into failure. If you can do it alone, then you already have the power for greatness.

Most importantly: Keep God first. He has your back and will make sure you will succeed. Don't let the media or rappers or the public make you think you are less than your worth. You are not a hoe, a bitch, or a Thot. Always remember that!

Fellas get out of:

- The house and go make some power moves.

- The clubs & strip clubs and go make it rain on opening some businesses in our communities.

- Street Gangs and into Mentoring programs to show our kids some guidance.

- Liquor and drugs and into healthy living. Get your mind right.

- Trapping, because that's exactly what it is, a "Trap" to get us locked up.

- The hood. Travel and go see the world.

Most importantly: Get out and go build a family, find yourself a good wife, and repair our broken homes.

Don't Buy What They're Selling

FYI, for my young dudes out there. Do not believe most of these rappers because they are not real. For example: William Roberts was a Dade County, FL Correctional Officer who stole the persona of Popular LA Drug Trafficker Ricky Ross and became Rick Ross.

Hip Hop is very powerful and they use these rappers to convey their message of terror upon us. They use hip hop for psychological warfare to keep us locked up, killing other brothers, trapping, degrading our women, and keeping us high so we won't focus on success.

If you don't believe me, turn on the radio and listen to which songs they are playing. Trap, Trap, Trap by Rick Ross, Molly Percocets by Future, and all kinds of things that have a negative impact on our lives. If you notice, there are no mainstream songs talk about building entrepreneurship, supporting each other, positivity, or becoming great.

The First 48

I am shaking my head at the things I see on *The First 48*. Instead of building with each other, we are killing each other for dumb stuff. We look like straight savages on that show.

We could lower the crime and the hating on each other if we learn to start getting real money by building businesses in our communities, learning how to generate income beside hustling or selling drugs, and setting examples that we don't have to depend on the streets or having a job to win. Our people swear the only path to riches is crime, a job, becoming a rapper, or becoming a ball player. That is why we are in last place financially.

Things To Remember:

- If your job sets you free....STAY FREE! It's just God telling you to go for your dreams.

- Education should not be a debt sentence.

- Be with someone who makes you feel like you hit the lottery every day when you wake up.

- The only time you should look back is to see how far you've come.

- No matter how hard life gets, remember, go to bed thankful that you have one.

- Old ways won't open new doors.

- Stop trying to fit in when you were born to stand out!

- Life is too short to be working for someone else's dream.

- Stop being afraid of what could go wrong and think of what could go right.

- Winners focus on winning, losers focus on winners.

- Sometimes the wrong choices bring us to the right places.

- Be strong but not rude.

- Be humble but not timid.

- Be proud but not arrogant.

- Be kind but not weak.

- If you never try, you'll never know.

- Sometimes the best therapy is a long drive and some great music!

- Nothing changes if nothing changes.

- You can't have million dollar dreams with a minimum wage work ethic.

- The purpose of a Woman in your life is to be your Motivator & Motivation.

- Within the word OWN is the word NOW.

- You don't need a fan club. All you need is to believe in your idea & invest in it.

- Spending more time at work than with your family is the real Pyramid Scheme.

- People don't buy WHAT you do...They buy WHY you do it!

- Be a Firm believer in stepping YOUR MOTHER FKN GAME UP!

- Your advice should come from people that MULTIPLY money.... Not just MAKE it.

- When doing BIG things there is absolutely no need to discuss with SMALL minds.

- Stop accepting everything that is below your worth. Jobs & friends included!

- Only 2% of programming on TV will help you become successful.

- "CAN'T" is the worst word ever created in the English language. Clear it from your vocabulary!

- If you can't find a job.......Hustle your butt off and make one!

- Always make a bold demand. Set your price high and do not waver.

Life Is Like a Camera

Life is like a camera

FOCUS on what's important,

CAPTURE the good times,

DEVELOP from the negatives,

And if things don't work out...take another shot!

Reality Shows We Need

I have a few reality shows to pitch while I'm out here in Hollywood, CA:

- Building an EMPIRE

- Love & Creating Wealth

- The Real Go-getters of Atlanta

We need REAL reality shows to show us how to build wealth, stop struggling, and how to get money. Forgot all that other ratchetness.

Beware The Playa

The brother on the LEFT is ONLY trying to get in your pants. He sees you as a hoe, a thot, a bitch, and a baby momma. He is NOT trying to build with you and NOT trying to grow old with you. If you have a kid with him, you will end up as a statistic that raises the child in a single household.

He sees you as just someone he can use for sex. He is a little boy in a grown man's body. Beware and stay far away from this type.

The brother on the RIGHT sees you as his queen. He treasures you and wants to spoil you. You are his motivation to become successful. He wants you to be his WIFE. He thinks the world of you, you are his

WHY, he will go all out to make both you and his dreams come true.

He wants to build a family and grow old with you.

Ladies learn to recognize a loser. Stop giving these little boys, clowns, and deadbeats the time of day. Find yourself a grown man that you can call your King.

Mindset

BROKEMINDED IS WHEN YOU SPEND 100% OF YOUR MONEY AND INVEST 0% INTO YOURSELF.

POOR IS

P.ASSING

O.VER

O.PPORTUNITIES

R.EPEATEDLY.

I remember a while back this interview manager gave me a gift of a company pen. He said if I wanted the job I would have to sell it back to him. So I got up out my seat and took his pen and put in my pocket and walked out the interview.

He chased me down the hallway and asked for his pen back. I told him he can keep the job I'm selling the pen on eBay for $50 along with a nice story of how I walked off the interview. The only way he could get his pen back was if he beat my eBay price and give me $51.

The look on his face was priceless. I got a job offer letter 2 hours later in my email.

Richminded Tip: Always out think the next person, act like a boss, and you will go very far in life.

Check Yourself

I wrote this book, Richminded, to help people build businesses. Why?

Because once upon a time, almost everybody in America owned their own businesses! Now, we basically own nothing.

Wall Street owns damn near every business in our neighborhoods and they rarely ever give you the jewels to do the same. Should we blame them for not giving up the secrets to success? NO!

But we could stop giving them so much of our money.

Should we blame the system for holding us back? NO!

Should we blame all the foreigners who come over here and bust their rearends to achieve their dreams? HELL NO!

We have to blame ourselves for spending all our money on dumb stuff, place blame upon ourselves for calling every opportunity for business a scam, place blame upon ourselves because we'd rather hate on people instead of collaborating and building with them.

Place blame on the fact that we are the most comfortable people on this planet. We'd rather build someone else's dreams and make others generational wealth than take some time and invest in ourselves to build our own.

It Isn't the Devil

People love to blame the devil for EVERYTHING!! There is something about placing blame for OUR ignorant actions that makes us feel good about our dumb decisions

"The devil just took my job!" "The Devil is a Liar"

Um....no....your attitude, your dishonesty, your decision to tell the boss off, and showing up late on a daily basis took your job. The fact that you are just a number to your employer and should be building your own companies took your job.

"The devil destroyed my marriage."

Uh.....no.....your failure to carry your financial weight as a man, staying out late at strip clubs, and treating your spouse like trash took out your marriage.

"The devil got me broke and struggling"

Um.....HELL no (no pun intended).

You thinking everything is a scam, never investing in yourself, being scared to death of making moves, and listening to bad advice from brokeminded people has got you broke & struggling.

"The devil got me single"

No...you wanting the perfect man, tall, dark, handsome, rich, no kids, college-educated, no baggage, perfect gentleman, light eyes, high credit score, and with a 6 pack has you single. You are looking for GOD!

The devil is a bad dude. I get all that......but STOP blaming him for YOUR ignorant decisions!!!!

When WE accept responsibility, then WE have the power to implement the necessary Richminded changes for success.

Brokeminded or Richminded?

The girl on the LEFT is a full-blown hater. She gossips about you and won't support you. She is jealous of your success and will prey on your downfall. She will take your man and has no goals in life. She has an attitude problem and will be nothing more than a baby momma.

She sits on social media watching your every move because she wants badly for you to fail. She terrorizes her baby daddy and is a terrible role model to her kids. She has no ambition in life, is on social media looking for attention, and she will not stop until you are as miserable as she is.

She is Brokeminded.

The woman on the RIGHT is about her business. She works to fund her dreams. Her family is everything to her. She wants to be a wife. She is down for her man. She won't settle for less. She has values, morals, and very high standards.

She is down-to-earth, she supports her friends and family, and she is going after success. She prays. She is a great mother and a role model to her kids. She wants everyone around her to win. She is making moves.

She is Richminded!

P.O.O.R.

Brokeminded is when you spend 100% of your money and Invest 0% Into Yourself. Poor is P.assing O.ver O.pportunities R.epeatedly.

Being Brokeminded leads to the 4 Devils: Lust • Envy • Hate • Jealousy

Be Careful With Words

Be careful of the words you speak into existence. Words are a "Spell" that is why they teach you to spell in school.

If you speak life into existence, you will get the best out of life.

When you speak death, then death will follow. Look at Biggie's albums for example: Life After Death, Ready 2 Die. Sadly, he got murdered.

When you speak brokenness, such as I'm poor, I'm broke, I'm struggling, I can't afford it, it won't work, I will fail, etc., then you will always remain broke.

When you speak wealth, then wealth will follow you.

Get certain words out of your vocabulary. Go hard to become great and become the OPPOSITE of what people expect you to be.

Moral of the Story: Choose your words carefully.

Society's Advice:

1. Go to school.

2. Get a debt sentence.

3. Go from job to job.

4. Work to pay off debts.

5. Retire at age 70.

6. DIE.

Richminded Advice:

1. Go to school if you want to.

2. Start a business.

3. Work your butt off and Hustle SMART.

4. Manifest your greatness.

5. Travel the world.

6. Surround yourself with bosses.

7. Create WEALTH for your family.

8. Retire at age 40.

9. LIVE.

I don't care how much your check says. You cannot put a price on freedom or creativity.

A Tale of Two Friends

A year ago I had conversations with two of my friends. The first one was with my boy Lever. I told him that he was worth a million dollars. I also told him that God gave him a gift to be great and to use it to build wealth and help others along the way.

But to him, entrepreneurship or anything not a job was a scam, fast money, a hustle, and lazy. He even made fun of me and called me Tommy from Martin.

He never took the advice and currently is still struggling. I tried, but his mind was too enslaved to a job.

I told the exact same thing to my boy Nate. But Nate's eyes and ears were all the way open. He was tired of getting bamboozled at his job and tired of giving away all his time in return for being broke and living check to check.

He listened and started following his dreams, using his gift for success, and making sure he earned what he felt he was worth. He went from making 30k a year to making 300k a year.

Moral of the Story: Better Nate than Lever.

A Tale of Two Friends, Part 2

Just got off the phone with my two good friends Nate and Lever. We all had a conversation on FB, Twitter, Instagram and YouTube.

Big difference on how they both used social media this year. Nate used these social media sites for building his brand, promoting his business, networking, making income and meeting likeminded people. He made over 6 figures with less than 3 hours a day on social media.

Lever told me he basically spends 3-5 hours a day on social media reading posts, cracking jokes, sharing funny videos and memes, sharing selfies, chasing women, being nosy, fake flossing, and telling all his everyday business. He made $0 from social media, but he did get a lot of likes.

Moral of the Story: Better Nate than Lever!

Think Like A Boss!

You can question yourself, be fearful, think somebody is trying to get one over on you, be scared to make a move, be frightened that you will lose money, and think somebody is out to get you. You can have full belief in your job and your boss and that you will never need extra income.

You can believe that Santa is going to put Christmas gifts under your tree every year, believe that the tooth fairy is going to put money under your pillow when you lose teeth, and believe every opportunity to win is a scam, but I promise you that you will remain broke and struggling, losing your mind, if you don't start thinking like a BOSS who is ready to win.

Change Your mindset

Change your mindset! Focus on winning, creating wealth, being around people that will uplift you, and spend less time on individuals or things that don't matter to your success. Make moves, know your worth, and make your haters your motivators.

Expand Your Beliefs

Have you ever noticed that brokeminded people only ask for days off and pay raises?

They never ask how someone built their business. Their limited realities won't allow them to dream big enough. Expand your beliefs and don't limit yourself to what you can accomplish!

Get Over Your Fear!

Fear was not a factor when you took out loans and went to school for 4-8 years to get a job based on a piece of paper.

Fear was not a factor when you sent your resume to 100 different companies to try to get an interview, not knowing if you would ever get a call back.

Fear was not a factor when you had to go to 3 different interviews and put on an academy award winning performance to impress the bosses so that you would even get considered for the job.

Fear wasn't even a factor when you finally got that offer letter and it was way below your worth. You just figured you would get by the best way you could.

So why is fear a factor when it's time to build and network, go after your own dreams, take a chance on creating wealth for your family and building your own businesses?

You Are A Product Of Your Choices

Growing up, Eric Thomas was the butt of everyone's jokes. Growing up, you might have been the butt of everyone's jokes.

No one ever took Eric Thomas seriously. Everyone treated him like trash. No one might have ever taken you seriously. They might have treated you like trash.

Eric Thomas lived in abandoned buildings, and ate out of garbage cans. You might have grown up struggling the same way.

Eric Thomas suffered from depression and hopelessness. You might have suffered from depression and hopelessness.

Eric Thomas is a self-made multi-millionaire, and the #1 speaker in the WORLD. You, right now, are not living in your purpose but you can be.

We are NOT victims of our circumstances. We are products of our CHOICES!

Turn Your Negatives Into A Positive

I'll give you 3 examples.

Example # 1 If you grew up poor and struggling, make sure your family never struggles. Keep a chip on your shoulder and decide that you will never put them in a position to be broke.

Always find creative ways to build generational wealth and hustle for success. Open your mindset, embrace opportunity, and go make that money.

Example # 2 If you lost a job recently, do whatever it takes to make sure you are NEVER in that predicament again. Use your gifts and talents and start creating your own job to build your own dreams so that the wealth you build can sustain you and no one has the power to stop your greatness. Use that job loss to open the powerful doors of financial freedom.

Example # 3 if you are currently unhappy, don't know where to turn to, depressed, don't have the answers, don't see the light at the end of the tunnel, or worried sick then pray to Him and ask Him to show you the way. He put those feelings into you so that you can make change, become great, not be scared, not have anything to lose and not have any fear whatsoever to take on the world.

This right here is a Billion Dollar Richminded Jewel. Turn that negative into a positive and you will be alright

Why We Fail

When it comes to a job: Hook me up, introduce me to the manager, let me know when they're hiring, pass them my resume, put me on, let them know I went to college for 4 years, tell your boss I'm a great worker, pray for me because I need those benefits, I'll do or pay whatever it takes to get the job.

When it comes to starting a business: It's too hard. Most businesses fail. I don't have any money. That's a scam. Only rich people start businesses. It's too much work. It will fail. Nobody will support me. I'd rather have a job. I need a guaranteed check every Friday.

And this is a brokeminded way of thinking. Having 10 different monthly bills, but only 1 stream of income, is why you will fail.

Don't Bash Them, Help Them!

You're saying if you clean up your associates, you'll clean up your influences. If you clean up your influences, you'll clean up your thinking. If you clean up your thinking, you'll clean up your life.

If you clean up your life, you'll clean up your outcomes. If you clean up your outcomes, you'll begin the process of accumulating lasting wealth, prosperity and a healthy, fulfilling life! Did I get that right?

Try a new approach. Don't bash them, help them!

Too many people we know really don't know anything other than being taught to go to school for 4-8 years and be in debt, use their degree to find a job, and basically live happily ever after. They turn their noses up at working for themselves, following their own dreams, and most all opportunities presented to them to do business, do better, or make change.

But this is all they know because this is what was taught to them by their family, friends, teachers, and their surroundings. You have to help them SEE the light at the end of the tunnel. That's how you will get your blessings and see your business grow.

Learn from the Thieves

During a robbery, the bank robber shouted to everyone in the bank: "Don't move. The money belongs to the state. Your life belongs to you."

Everyone in the bank laid down quietly. This is called a "Mind Changing Concept." They were changing the conventional way of thinking.

When a lady lay on the table provocatively, the robber shouted at her: "Please be civilized! This is a robbery and not a rape!"

This is called "Being Professional." Focus only on what you are trained to do!

When the bank robbers returned home, the younger robber who was very smart told the older robber, who was not as smart "Big brother, let's count how much we got."

The older robber rebutted and said: "You are very stupid. There is so much money it will take us a long time to count. Tonight, the TV news will tell us how much we robbed from the bank!"

This is called "Experience." Nowadays, experience is more important than paper qualifications!

After the robbers left, the bank manager told the bank supervisor to call the police quickly. But the supervisor said to him: "Wait! Let us take out $10 million from the bank for ourselves and add it to the $70 million that we have previously embezzled from the bank".

This is called "Swim with the tide." Convert an unfavorable situation to your advantage!

The supervisor says: "It will be good if there is a robbery every month."

This is called "killing boredom." Personal happiness is more important than your job.

The next day, the TV news reported that $100 million was taken from the bank. The robbers counted and counted and counted, but they could only count $20 million. The robbers were very angry and complained: "We risked our lives and only took $20 million. The bank manager took $80 million with a snap of his fingers. It looks like it is better to be educated than to be a thief!"

This is called "Knowledge is worth as much as gold!"

The bank manager was smiling and happy because his losses in the share market are now covered by this robbery.

This is called "Seizing the opportunity." Daring to take risks!

95% of you are doing jobs that you hate and are underpaid for.

You have to stop doing things that are keeping you miserable and living paycheck-to-paycheck. You have to stop letting these jobs steal 20 hours a day from you building someone else's dreams. If you don't think it's 20 hours a day let me break it down.

6am - 7am get ready for work

7am - 8am drive to work

8am - 5pm actually work

5pm - 6pm drive home from work

10pm - 6am 8 hours of sleep in preparation for work = 20 hours a day.

You barely get 4 hours a day to yourself!!!

All you are thinking about is work, work, work. I don't know which teacher or family member taught you that building someone else's dreams would make you happy and successful, but they were wrong. I know people that have been working for 5,10,15, and 20 years but barely have $100 to their name.

You have to stop this madness now. I'm not telling you to quit your jobs, but what I am saying is you have to start hustling your gifts and talents for success and prepare a business model so you can eventually free yourself from others controlling your time and how you spend your life. It's not too late to change directions.

You can't complain about being hungry if you are not seizing every opportunity to eat.

Dont worry about failing!

F.A.I.L = First Attempt In Learning

The end is never the end!

E.N.D = Effort Never Dies

If you get no as an answer always remember:

N.O = Next Opportunity

True Story

Sometimes you just have to let go. Whatever is stressing you out in life, let it go. Whether it's a job, a business that's failing, a significant other, your friends and family or your surroundings, let it go and focus on YOU and your success. That's how you win.

Money

THE GOAL ISN'T MORE MONEY.

THE GOAL IS LIVING LIFE ON YOUR TERMS.

Don't start a business because you are desperate for the money. Start because you are committed to success.

Spend R.I.C.H., Live R.I.C.H.

You have money for:

- Designer Clothes
- Weed
- Red Bottoms & Jordans
- Weaves
- Rims
- The Club
- Apple or Samsung
- A 60 inch TV
- Popping Bottles
- Tricking
- Gambling

But you always have excuses when it comes to investing in yourself. Stop spending every last dollar you have on things that will not help you advance and create wealth. That's a poverty mindset!

The Goal

The goal isn't more money. The goal is living life on your terms. Holding on to money and having an emotional attachment to it is a poverty mindset.

It's Easy To Be A Millionaire

Everyone wants to be a millionaire, but very few understand that it is simple to get there!

Option 1. Get 5,000 people to buy a $200 product.

Option 2. Get 2,000 people to buy a $500 product.

Option 3. 1,000 people to buy a $1000 product.

Option 4. 500 people to buy a $2000 product.

Option 5. $300 people to buy a $3,333 product.

Can't sell a product? No problem, just sell a service!

Option 6. Get 5,000 people to pay $17 a month, for 12 months.

Option 7. Get 2,000 people to pay $42 a month, for 12 months.

Option 8. Get 1,000 people to pay $83 a month, for 12 months.

Option 9. Get 500 people to pay $167 a month, for 12 months.

Option 10. Get 300 people to pay $278 a month, for 12 months.

I just gave you 10 different options, so there are literally no excuses!

"I'm Broke"

The two words you can use as MOTIVATION or as an EXCUSE.

Opportunity

USE YOUR TIME AT WORK TO STUDY THE BOSS, THE SYSTEM, THE WAY THE BUSINESS WORKS, HOW EMPLOYEES MOVE, AND HOW YOUR JOB PROFITS.

This is how you have fun at your job and make the time go faster. Use your time at work to study the boss, the system, the way the business works, how employees move, and how your job profits. Study every day. Class is in session every day that you go to work on how to build your own empire.

The Internet Is Rich With Opportunities

Marques Brownlee is the very essence of being Richminded. This young brother is only 23-years old. He created a YouTube channel and just started randomly posting product reviews. He reviews everything from cameras, phones, and other electronic gadgets to new cars.

He now has more than 4.5 million subscribers, and he earns $3 MILLION per year!!!!!! If that's not Richminded I don't know what else is!

Make Your Brand a Social Media Success

The 8 major social media accounts you can use to make your brand successful:

• YouTube has 1 billion active users every month

• Facebook has 1.9 billion active users every month

• Twitter has 315 million active monthly users

• Instagram has 600 million active monthly users

• Snapchat has has 7 billion views daily

• Google+ has 2.2 billion users

• LinkedIn has 467 million users.

• Pinterest has 100 million monthly active users

Make sure you have an account with each. There are plenty of consumers out there. You just have to be Richminded and go get 'em! Don't let any one stop you, and don't let any miserable souls try and kill your dreams.

Pray

EVERY NIGHT, NO MATTER HOW YOUR DAY WENT, YOU SHOULD ALWAYS READ, PRAY, AND REFLECT ON THE DAY.
LIE DOWN ON A POSITIVE NOTE, AND PICTURE TOMORROW'S SUCCESS.

Just pray and ask God to help you become successful. That's the 1st step. All you have to do is keep pushing, keep praying, and keep going. Practice makes perfect. Things may not be at the level you want right now, but in time it will be.

Pray the Richminded Way

Let me show you how to pray the Richminded way.

If you ask God for strength, he will give you difficulties to make you strong.

If you ask Him for wisdom, He will give you problems to solve.

If you ask Him for prosperity, He will give you the brains and energy to put in that work.

If you ask Him for courage, He will give you dangers to overcome.

If you ask Him for patience, he will place you in situations where you ARE FORCED TO WAIT.

If you ask Him for love, He will give you troubled people to help.

If you ask Him for favors, He will present opportunities to become successful.

If you ask for everything so that you can enjoy life, He will give you life so that you can enjoy everything.

You will receive nothing you want from Him, but EVERYTHING you need.

Purpose

STOP STRESSING AND EMBRACE THE STRUGGLE.

OPEN YOUR MIND.

IN ORDER TO BE SUCCESSFUL, YOU'VE GOT TO FEEL THE PAIN FIRST.

Embrace everything wrong that's going on in your life right now because all it's doing is leading you to your purpose. Doors are closing for more to open, people are going out your life to make room for other people that will lead you to your destiny, and you are struggling because its moving you away from being comfortable.

Stop stressing and embrace the struggle. Open your mind. In order to be successful, you've got to feel the pain first.

You Can Do So Much Better

That door that is shutting in your face is pointing you towards another. You might get fired continuously from a job, or keep having issues with management, but pay attention to yourself. This is a mirror the universe is showing you. You can do so much better than what you've been signing yourself up for.

You're probably destined for greatness but you cut yourself short, because either you don't see it clearly yet, or you do but fear is holding you hostage. Get rid of the fear and you will see amazing things happen believe that!

Tell Your Story

Tell your story and tell it often. You never know who might be listening from some of the same conditions, and/or circumstances that you once lived in.

You never know who might draw the inspiration to get back up and to give it one more shot after hearing from you. You never know who might be in despair and possibly considering suicide.

You never know who might be looking at you and thinking: Wow! If he/she went through this and made it out, then SO CAN I!!

Success

DREAMS DON'T WORK UNLESS YOU GO ALL OUT FOR SUCCESS.

SOMEBODY, SOMEWHERE IS DEPENDING ON US TO HELP THEM SEE THE VISION OF SUCCESS.

Dreams don't work unless you go all out for success. Somebody, somewhere is depending on us to help them see the vision of success.

Don't Let Someone Else Determine Your Success

I'm an avid watcher of the NBA draft every year. I remember when Steph Curry got drafted like it was yesterday. He was picked #7. The GM's picked 6 other people in front of him. 2 of them are not even the NBA today.

Some of these well-paid world-renowned talent scouts said he was too small, he couldn't shoot at an NBA level, he came from a small school, he would be a bench player, he is half the player his dad was. He proved them all wrong and is one of the best ever on one of the best teams ever.

Moral of the Story: Don't ever let another person determine how successful you will be. Just let them hate and let them watch the greatness unfold. Success is the best payback you can give a hater. Don't let their words stop you ever!

Keys To Success

Hard work won't guarantee success, but it will greatly improve your chances! Go hard to become successful or spend the rest of your life working hard for someone who does. The path to success is to take massive, determined action.

If you're not 100% in, you will fail. You don't have to be great to get started, you just have to get started to be great! You will see success when you stop selling people and start helping people.

Focus on Success

Ignore the negativity, stupidity, and toxicity. Focus on becoming successful. Let go of anything that is toxic to your progression! Your mindset will determine your success.

Your new life is going to cost you your old one. It is impossible to reach new levels, while holding on to old habits.

Stay away from negative people. They have a problem for every solution. Whoever is trying to bring you down is already below you.

Hang out with people who force you to level up. Get around people you can build with, not just chill with!

Stop Playing and Build for Success

From this point on, just tell yourself that as of today there are no more excuses, no more holding back, no more hypnotizing myself into believing that you will fail, no more listening to dream killers even if it's people you love, no more fear, and no more giving up your valuable time for anything way below your worth. Whatever happened in the past is over. Time to stop playing and build for success.

Average People Don't Succeed

Want to know how long it takes for the average person to have success?

Answer: The average person does not succeed. So, if you want to succeed, do not be average.

Be the type of person that when your feet touch the floor in the morning, the devil says "Awww, shit. They're up." - Dwayne The Rock Johnson

Focus on Serving Others and Success Will Follow

Successful people are always looking for opportunities to help others. Unsuccessful people are always asking "What's in it for me?"

You should not need compensation or incentive to help people. You should genuinely want to help people whether you get paid or not!

Everyone wants to become "rich" overnight. There is no one giant step that leads to success. It is a lot of little steps that will get you there.

Life is about making an impact, not making an income. You will be remembered by the lives you impact, not by how much money you made.

Success Depends on U

Success all depends on the second letter, U. I can give U the tools, the guidance and will always help U along the way, but it's up to U to put in the effort and time. I can't do that for U.

Most people are willing to spend $100,000 and 4 years of their life to learn a skill set, where there is no guarantee they ever use it or make money using from it. Yet, most people won't spend a few hours a week learning a skill set that they can use to make money at anytime and anywhere in the world?

Be Ready

If you are going to become successful you have to become READY!

- Ready to take on the world.

- Ready to go all out after your dreams.

- Ready to lose envious jealous friends.

- Ready to put in hard work and energy that will pay off.

- Ready to brand yourself and not others.

- Ready for financial change.

- Ready to control your time & future.

- Ready to finally build on what you are really worth.

Stay On Point

It shouldn't take you losing nearly everything for you to get back on point and on top of your shit... Stay on point at all times. Especially when you are doing good.

The Go-Getters Schedule

Tuesday: Thinking BIG!

Networking, Building, Researching, Making Income. Our dreams and goals have us thinking BIG.

Monday: Preparing our week for making income and networking.

Very busy day thinking about our dreams. Positive thoughts focused on success and wealth throughout the day.

Wednesday: Hump Day.

Networking, Building, Researching, Making Income. Our mindset is getting stronger and more powerful by the hour.

Thurs: Grind Mode.

Networking, Building, Researching, Making Income. In grind mode preparing for the weekend.

Fri: Enjoying Friday and ready to turn up from our week-long ambitions.

Focused on upcoming projects, building a wider circle of like minded friends and networking with winners.

Sat: Our chill out day.

Shopping, exploring, hanging out and time with family. Income flows while we spend time doing us

Sun: OFF

Church, Family, Reading, Relaxing, Sunday Dinner, and thinking of ways to be creative & grow. Cannot hardly rest because our dreams are growing so much and we have so much ambition for growth. We are excited for what's in store for the upcoming week.

The Lottery Is No Success Strategy

Fun fact if you're looking to quit your job! The lottery gives you a 1 in 292 million chance of quitting your job. Starting a business gives you a 1 in 10 chance of quitting your job.

Most people choose to play the lottery instead because they have no faith in themselves and they think wealth is all about luck. In the dictionary, and in life, sacrifice will always come before success!

You won't get abs with 1 crunch. You can't build muscle with 1 rep. You won't lose 10 pounds with 1 mile. You can't have a relationship with 1 date. You can't build a fortune in 1 day

The results you want don't happen until you've fought for them day after day after day. Consistent action creates consistent results! If someone tells you that you can't do it, it really means that they are just afraid to see you succeed

Your strongest muscle is your mind! Just like any muscle, if you don't use it, it will weaken. If you don't use your mind, it will fail. Train it well.

If you do not go after what you want, you'll never have it. If you do not ask, the answer will always be no. If you do not step forward, you will always be in the same place.

Don't Be An Askhole

AskHOLE - Keeps asking you for advice to become successful but never does anything.

Support

Haters don't really hate you...They hate themselves because you are a reflection of what they wish they could be.

First they watch, then they hate, then they copy.

I saw a beautiful picture of a bride kissing her groom. Behind that groom were six men whose arms were linked together. The groom was paralyzed and his friends were helping him to stand up so he could have that moment. This is the meaning of support.

Friends should uplift you, support you, be there for you, and Hustle SMART with you. No matter what. No excuses.

If you need $100, they shouldn't ask what you need it for, they should ask when do you need it by. If they see you putting out your goals and dreams they should do whatever it takes to help you see success. That's a real friend. Both in the Facebook world, and also in the real world.

Be Careful

Watch out for miserable people. They will get into your soul if you let them.

You have people bashing religion, people that constantly talk about their political views, people that are always showing off or faking success. You have people that show up to troll you and disagree with you, people that will not support you no matter what, people that are racist (black or white), people that are negative, people that seek attention, people that are around just to watch your every move, and people that try to kill your dreams. They are all around you.

Be very careful which people you let in your circle. Try to rock with people who are all about success, that help uplift you and also about helping others

Don't Worry About the Haters

Don't worry about the haters, non-supporters, and dream killers in your life. These crabs are all present for a reason.

Haters don't really hate you...They hate themselves because you are a reflection of what they wish they could be. First they watch, then they hate, then they copy.

We are going to keep them around just so that they can witness our rise & success. Let their ignorance motivate you into greatness. The world is yours. Be Richminded and go get that success.

Watch Out

Watch out for people who you call family or friend. They will tell you it can't be done, you are too old, or it will never work. They will give you the side eye when you go after success. They will ignore your posts on your dreams and goals.

They will only support you if it's building up someone else's dreams and they will encourage you to follow the normal, safe routine. They will say snide remarks like "9 out of 10 businesses fail," or "It's too much work. Get a real job," or "Entrepreneurship is not for everyone," or "It's not realistic," or "It's a scam." They will make all kinds of fear-based statements to hold you back from greatness.

Be careful who you listen to. The devil is real. Fear is evil.

Who Cares?

If they don't support you, who cares? There are a billion consumers out there!

Parents

I always hear these parents in our communities say "I'm so proud they going to college" or "I'm so proud they got this job" but I never hear them say, "I'm so proud they opened their own business" or "I'm so proud they building their own dreams."

Stop that!

It's time you go all out to help your kids create wealth, too. Think beyond just going to college, getting in debt, and looking for a job. These streets are real. Stop handicapping them.

Build a Wealth Club

Every week you and a few friends should get together by phone, in person, or video chat to cross reference ideas, help uplift each other, brainstorm, vent, pray with each other, and network to build wealth for you and your families.

Trust that you cannot build an empire on your own. Having like-minded go-getters exchanging ideas will help you go a long way. Call it your weekly wealth club.

Build a Great Circle of Facebook Friends

Use social media to your advantage when building a circle of friends. If you are surrounded by 9 brokeminded people, you will be the 10th.

Too many of you care what others think. That right there keeps you struggling. We have all this technology and social media to create brands, build empires, and start businesses but because you don't want to look thirsty, or look like you are in need, or have the fear of rejection you use it to talk about food, the weather, sports, celebs, music and random thoughts to appease people who wouldn't rub two nickels together to support you.

Most of your friends and family look down on business and entrepreneurship and going after success because they don't have the heart, the vision, or the shine to make dreams possible and that is why you hardly ever see support from them.

But stop trying to appease them and get their validation.

You gotta STOP that. START doing you.

Show your dreams, your goals, your business, your links, your talents and your gifts. Do it for YOU. The hell with them. Show what's on your heart and don't worry about fitting in with people who not on the same level as you.

Real Talk.

Get Some Real Friends

Real friends support everything you do even if they don't see the vision.....YET

Real friends have your back in your time of need. If you need something they don't ask "Why" or say things like "I can't " they say things like "I got you" or "what you need?" They make a way to help you.

Real friends uplift you. When you are feeling down, they are feeling up. When you are weak, they are strong, and vice versa.

Real friends want to see you win and win big. No hate, no shade, no jealousy. No praying on your downfall. They want you as successful as you can be.

A real friend sees when no one likes, shares, or interacts with your posts about goals, dreams, aspirations, positivity, success, and being about your business and is right there sharing, liking, and in the comments section supporting you to the fullest. That's a REAL friend!

Your bosses, managers, gm's, and the higher ups at your job are not your friends! They will fire you and ruin your life quickly and feel no remorse about it. Stop putting these people on pedestals and put some faith into yourself to do big things. You can do whatever you want and be as successful as you want to be if you put as much focus on building your dreams as you do impressing the people who hire and fire you.

Look for People Who Offer Real Solutions

When you lose your job all they tell you is this: "Things happen for a reason," or, "The devil is a liar," or, " When one door closes another one will open," or "I'm praying for you," or "Send me your resume."

They never give you a real solution like "I'll help you push through," or, "Here is a few dollars. I'll help you start your own business so you can create your own income," or give you some real positive thoughts to change your mindset from depending on others. Look for people who offer real solutions. They're your real friends.

If they didn't support you in in the past why are you still holding on to them in the present.

This year is about to be on fire for you. Let them go, because they are stopping your greatness. Replace them with people that will go through the struggle with you, who want to build with you, support you, uplift you, make you feel special, and give you words of wisdom. I promise you will feel 1000% better without people that don't support your dreams in your life. They are sideways haters anyway.

Be a Lifeguard

I took my kids to the pool inside the hotel and let them swim. I decided to move closer to the pool since I didn't want them going in the deeper part so I sat in the lifeguard's chair to watch them. My 6-year-old daughter asks me if I'm the lifeguard.

I started cracking up and told her, "No, daddy's not the lifeguard." But then it hit me, and I thought to myself, "Maybe I am a lifeguard. I'm always trying to help people who are drowning and giving them fresh air. Drowning in debt, drowning in misery over their jobs and finances, needing to breathe again, facing their fears and learning how to swim etc."

So, I guess I am a lifeguard. And a damn good one at that!

We are all lifeguards if we support our people, never let them drown, help them breath new air, keep them away from sharks and teach them the best way to swim when they are sinking.

You Are The Company You Keep!

If you hang around 4 people who hustle their butt off, you will be the 5th.

If you hang with 4 confident go-getters, you will be the 5th

If you hang around 4 intelligent winners, you will be the 5th

If you keep 4 millionaires in your circle, you will be the 5th

If you hang around 4 negative dreamkillers, you will be the 5th

Avoid People With STD's

Truth be told, I got rid of a lot of my old friends because of their STD. They were SCARED TO DEATH of thinking outside the box, following their dreams and being above average. If you wanna know your FUTURE...look at the people around you.

Get far away from anyone in your life that has a STD. If they are SCARED TO DEATH of thinking outside the box, following their dreams and being above average, then they have no reason to be in your circle.

Don't Get Distracted

Q: Do you know why racehorses wear blinders?

A: So they don't get distracted by horses that aren't in their lane.

Don't get distracted by haters, non-supporters, and people who are negative and miserable. They are not in the same lane as you. Keep pushing forward to success and keep those blinders on blocking out those who stand in your way.

Why They Don't Support You

People are not supporting you because you are really not giving them something to actually support. You are standing still, afraid of putting your dreams out there and making moves, because you don't want to look a certain way in your front of family and friends on social media.

You also put in 40-50 hours weekly for others but not even 1 hour for yourself to build and grow. You have to change that mindset. Then, people will get inspired and support you.

It's About To Get Ugly.

This year is about to be over and it's about to get real ugly next year. It's time to focus, stop b.s.'ing and stop trying to impress people. Get rid of toxic people and dream killers. Stop putting all your faith in jobs and your business on social media.

Amazon is about to kill jobs in the retail industry with their 30 minute drones. Self-serving kiosks are popping up all over the place. Unemployment is high and these companies are downsizing or outsourcing. It's time to stop playing games, start building businesses, and go all out for success.

Look back on all the struggling you did this year. Look at the hurt, the worry, the creditors, the paychecks you received that you know in your heart you were worth 100x more, the low bank account you had for the majority of the year, all the dreamkillers in your ear, the pride you had to swallow, the haters you had to deal with, and the lessons you had to learn. USE THOSE. Carry a chip on your shoulder. Become great. Become successful. Prove these no-getters and everyone who ever doubted you wrong in 2017.

Right now, many of you are going to a job that underpays you and makes you physically sick. You are stressed the f** out because you are struggling. You're robbing Peter to pay Paul, messing up your credit to survive, overdrawing your account, surviving on pennies to your next payday, and worried because every bill is hanging over your head.

But it doesn't have to be like that. Get out of your comfort zone and make some moves. Don't let anybody tell you that it's impossible, it won't work, quit, give up, go back to building other people's dreams. Don't let anybody tell you that you have to drive a broken down car, that you can't live where you want to live, that you can't be the best you can be, that you can't build your own dreams. Stop being scared to go after success.

Real talk....

If you want success and a better life, you have to remove and disassociate yourself with negative, unsupportive, brokeminded, ignorant, dreamkilling, skeptical, jealous, scared to go after success, always gossiping, always worshiping celebs, always hating, always blaming others for their failues, backstabbing, closeminded, insecure, judgmental, lazy, narcissistic, limited thinkers. Get rid of them!

You have to build with people who think BIG, who want to help & uplift you , who have goals & dreams and who want to be the best they can be. That's how you win.

Take 5 Seconds To Support Others

Every day I want you to go on social media and when you see somebody trying to do big things, simply type in their comments box:

"I believe in your dreams. Stay focused and you will be successful"

or

"I support you. I love what you're doing. Keep up the great work!" and hit like.

We should all support each other while we are trying to attain our dreams. All it takes is 5 seconds.

Support your friends, listen to their ideas, go to their events, share their posts, celebrate their victories, and always remind them of their importance after their failures.

A little support goes a looooooooong way!

Support Your People

Your family & friends should be speaking life into you. They should be in your spirit with positive energy. They should be hitting you up saying things like:

- Congrats on your success.

- I want to see you win.

- I hope you are a success.

- I want to help you or collaborate with you.

- I love what you are doing. How can I support you?

This is the type of energy we need to be flowing to each other. We should not just hear positivity from strangers but from the ones we love, been down for, would go to war for ,or the ones we would give the shirts off our back to.

Moral of the Story: Stop hating and support your people.

Support Your Own

A person starts a business and gets friends & family who

- offer barely any support.

- offer lust, hate, envy, and jealousy.

- always want discounts.

• would rather shop with other people.

This hurts all of us when we don't support each other. We gotta do better. We support other people every day, why not support our own as well?

Time

IF IT DOESN'T MAKE YOU MONEY, MAKE YOU BETTER, OR MAKE YOU HAPPY, YOU DON'T MAKE TIME FOR IT!

RICHMINDED

Tired of being broke? Stop wasting time doing things that don't make you money. Get to the point in life that if it doesn't make you money, make you better, or make you happy, you don't make time for it! Don't ever be jealous of anyone. Be inspired! We all get the same 24 hours to grind!

Are you trying to build wealth or waste time and energy?

People are so concerned with hating, slandering each other, trolling, being jealous, trying to outdo each other, getting over on each other, looking better in the eyes of others, balling more than the next person, preying on the downfall of others, worrying about what others think, building other people dreams, worrying about celebs, TV, and everything else that does not build their bank accounts that they are missing their calling, wasting their talents, and not developing their gifts.

Be careful what you feed your mind every day. Nevermind the TV or radio. The REAL BEAST is social media. People post fake news stories from fake sites, making you believe it's true.

The thirst for attention with girls showing everything that only should be reserved for your significant other. People are bragging like they are not in the struggle when they are really broke or don't have real bills and responsibilities.

People are constantly posting disrespectful memes. People share fight videos of our people looking crazy and all kinds of negativity. People waste time and energy sharing their opinions about Trump, Hilary, or random celebs who are already rich.

People make racist posts and comments not realizing these words can be captured in a screenshot and used against them. They post all kinds of craziness and all kinds of everyday nonsense that will distort your mind from building, creating, investing, saving, teaching, mentoring, family values, and living out your purpose. Be careful. The devil is real on here.

Ladies....Make social media about BUSINESS. Likes, comments, and inbox messages do not validate who you are as a person nor does it equal money.

If you are constantly putting up selfies or videos of yourself and get nothing but thirsty men trying to holla at you, then that's on you. You are going to spend valuable time ignoring, replying, and putting these dudes on inbox seen, ducking these guys like bill collectors, all because you want attention.

With all that energy, your focus could be on building a business and yourself an empire online. Time is very valuable. Change your mindset. Especially if you are struggling.

The 5 By 5 Rule

If it's not going to matter in 5 years, don't spend more than 5 minutes being upset by it!

Today

TODAY IS A NEW DAY.

YOU HAVE NEVER LIVED **THIS** DAY BEFORE.

YOU HAVE NOT MADE **ANY** MISTAKES
TODAY.

YOU HAVE **NO** REGRETS FROM **TODAY.**

Today is a new day. You have never lived THIS day before. You have not made ANY mistakes TODAY. You have NO regrets from TODAY.

(You) "Yeah, but yesterday and last week I......"

Quiet, Zip it. Shhhhh....and listen.

The other day is BEHIND us, and we are not going to carry the mistakes, failures, and/or disappointments of the other day or last week, or last month, or last year day into TODAY.

TODAY represents a NEW and a FRESH opportunity for each one of us to do things the RIGHT way! Today we can tackle the fear of building our own businesses, today is the day we stop competing and start collaborating, today is the day we no longer will accept anything below our worth and today is the day we look to build our future and put the past behind us.

Where You Are Today:

Being underpaid at your Job

Stressed from not seeing family

Morning Traffic

No time to build your dreams

Answering to a Boss

Where You Can Be Tomorrow:

Building your own dreams

Financial Freedom

Getting Paid what your worth

Big Paychecks from your hustle

Spending all the time you want with family

Life Tip:

Spending today complaining about yesterday won't make tomorrow any better. There are seven days in the week and "some day" isn't one of them. Follow your dreams! Start today!

If you are really serious about making 6 figures, building wealth, having nice things, not being stressed about your job, having savings, having credit, having a circle of friends that have your back and helping others around you, then you need to get off your ass and stop holding yourself back from greatness.

Broke Mindset:

Excuse 1 - I don't have the money.

Truth: You have money for Jordan's, Gucci, Cable TV, Red Bottoms, The Club, or an upgrade on a new Smartphone.

Excuse 2 - I don't have the time.

Truth: You give your job 10-14 hours a day.

Excuse 3 - I don't have the patience.

Truth: You have patience for traffic, a boss, coworkers, and low pay.

Excuse 4 - I'm going to do it someday.

Truth: No, you won't. Someday is not a day of the week.

Excuse 5 - If I have to invest in myself, it must be a Scam.

Truth: The real scam is low pay and never being able to spend time with your family.

Excuse 6 - I'm not good at selling.

Truth: You sold yourself at the interview for your job with the performance of a lifetime.

Excuse 7 - I can't because it will interfere with my welfare or disability.

Truth: That's a bum mindset.

Excuse 8 - My boss will find out.

Truth: Your Boss is not your master, nor does he or she control you. Slavery ended many years ago.

Excuse 9 - I'm SCARED I will fail.

Truth: Not if you believe in yourself and hustle hard for success.

Excuse 10 - My family and friends won't approve.

Truth: Forget what they think. Use the purpose and talent God gave YOU!

Do What Others Won't

Today, you have to do what others won't so that tomorrow you can do what others can't.

Richminded Conclusion

IF YOU NEED HELP FIXING YOUR CREDIT, BUILDING YOUR BUSINESS, NEED TRAINING ON HOW TO MASTER BEING SUCCESSFUL, NEED BUSINESS FUNDING, OR WANT YOUR CHILDREN TO BECOME **R**ICHMINDED AND TAUGHT ENTREPRENEURSHIP YOU CAN LOG ONTO WWW.RICHMINDED.NET AND WE WILL GO HARD FOR SUCCESS TOGETHER.

I want to close this book by telling you that can be very successful! No matter the odds, no matter how many brokeminded people tell you that you won't win or can't win, no matter how little money you have right now, no matter what happened yesterday, last week, last month, or last year and no matter how much time has passed with you struggling. All that doesn't even matter!!!

If you start believing in yourself and start going hard everyday working on your empire, I promise it will all pay off. If you need help fixing your credit, building your business, need training on how to master being successful, need business funding, or want your children to become Richminded and taught entrepreneurship you can log onto www.richminded.net and we will go hard for success together.

We support your dream, want to see you succeed, and want the highest possible level of success for you. Drop us an email, call or follow us on social media, and we will help you achieve your dreams of financial freedom.

COMING SOON! Richminded Kids

Richminded Kids will help build your child's mindset into the best success story possible. This blueprint for success manual is key to ensuring your young entrepreneur is constantly thinking big and will help change their mindset into greatness. This book will help them create their own income, manufacture their own meaning, and generate their own motivation. Richminded kids will help them pursue their passions, develop their creativity, and find their gifts.

Not only is it highly engaging, it is also a very fun read. This book is the quintessential component to early success and will empower our young adults to activate and develop their ideas, build entrepreneurial skills, and grow their confidence like never before.

About the Author

CONNECT WITH RASHAN ONLINE

TWITTER & INSTAGRAM:

@IAMRICHMINDED

FACEBOOK:

WWW.FACEBOOK.COM/RICHMINDEDMOVEMENT

WEBSITE:

HTTP://WWW.RICHMINDED.NET

Rashan Lawhorne is an author, speaker, motivational coach, father, mentor, and entrepreneur. His passion lies within motivating others to become Richminded and going all out for their dreams.

After losing multiple jobs, struggling, and almost losing his freedom due to the streets, he realized the power of entrepreneurship and financial freedom. He started Richminded Academy and the Young Entrepreneurs Network to convey his message of success.

Rashan wants us all to become Richminded so that we can spend more time with our families and create generational wealth.

Made in the USA
Columbia, SC
10 July 2018